CQ: THE LEGACY
LEADER'S SUPERPOWER

Driving Cultural Intelligence from
the Boardroom to the Mailroom

ANTHONY LOPEZ

WESTBOW
PRESS®
A DIVISION OF THOMAS NELSON
& ZONDERVAN

WestBow Press books may be ordered through booksellers or by contacting:

WestBow Press
A Division of Thomas Nelson & Zondervan
1663 Liberty Drive
Bloomington, IN 47403
www.westbowpress.com
844-714-3454

ISBN: 978-1-6642-7786-1 (sc)
ISBN: 978-1-6642-7788-5 (hc)
ISBN: 978-1-6642-7787-8 (e)

Library of Congress Control Number: 2022916890

Print information available on the last page.

WestBow Press rev. date: 09/22/2022

DEDICATION

This is for my family. My dad, Hector L. López Sr., who still teaches and guides me. My brother, Hector L. López Jr., who challenges me to be better. Yvette, who has supported and accompanied me in my life journey, even when I was hard to be with. Cristina and Marisa, who gave my life purpose. And to Madelyn Isabela, Maxwell Anthony, and Alexander James, who motivate me each day to want to be a better Papa and leave a legacy they will be proud of one day. This is also for my mom. I've tried to be a good man, Mom, and I hope I've made you proud. I miss you more each day.

PRAISE FOR

CQ: The Legacy Leader's Superpower

"I have known Tony for long enough to know that when he writes, I read. This book is a resource that will help us unlock the potential within each of us. Read it, apply it, and change the world around you. It will be time well spent!"

Chester Elton
Best-selling author of *Leading with Gratitude*

"Complex, diverse, global, and interdependent—that's the world leaders lead in today. Cultural intelligence is a must-have competency for the leader of today who wants to build for tomorrow. This gem of a book by my friend Tony Lopez will enable our journey to becoming better leaders."

Ivan Tornos
Chief operating officer
Zimmer Biomet

"Changing a paradigm requires a different approach. DE&I initiatives have been missing a fundamental ingredient to creating sustainable change in organizations. Cultural intelligence is that missing link, and in this book, Tony provides a road map for leaders to make a real difference in themselves and their organizations."

Eric Guerin
EVP, chief financial officer at CDK Global
Natus and Skyworks boards of directors

"Simple and fun to read, with an important message! This book will challenge us to rethink our DE&I strategies and guides leaders on how to develop and leverage cultural intelligence as a foundational skill to create organizations that deliver impressive results."

Diego G. Silva, MD, PhD
VP, Immunology Medical Affairs
Bristol Myers Squibb

"Lopez does a masterful job of showing how developing an organization's cultural intelligence unlocks the collective potential of its people, and the critical role leaders play in doing so. This is the right book for right now."

Tim Morin, president and CEO
WJM Associates, Inc., a global executive coaching company

"Straightforward and provocative, with a profound message for personal change and improvement. This book will change how we think about DE&I in the workplace, and how we can transform ourselves and our organizations into places that don't just talk about diversity but live it and leverage it every day in an organic way."

Janine Ting Jansen, Diversity, Equity & Inclusion leader
Organon, Inc

"There is one thing that I know about Tony Lopez, what he knows about world leadership and cultural intelligence doesn't just come from the many years as a strong leader, but from his heart. This is the kind of knowledge that can't be taught unless you first experience it. Thank you, Tony, for another great leadership book on a subject all of us need to embrace."

Daniel Gutierrez
International best-selling author, speaker, mindful leadership expert
Director/owner of Catalina Retreat Center in San Salvador, Peru

"*CQ: The Legacy Leader's Superpower* emphasizes the importance of cultural intelligence and how to refine our leadership skills with practical guidance to enable stronger teams. Tony well articulates that, beyond simply identifying diversity, leaders must work to leverage it as a true competitive advantage. To do this, they must embark on their own personal journey towards becoming more culturally intelligent and create organizations with high CQ teams. This book is an excellent resource to help leaders embrace unique differences embodied in their teams and enable them to drive sustainable future growth in the organizations they are privileged to lead."

Jocelyn M. Petersen
Chief financial officer, Capacity LLC

"Tony Lopez lays out a terrific case for cultural intelligence. It is thoughtful, insightful and creates a roadmap as to what comes next with DE&I. An underlying thought in his book is a clear message that leadership is important but learning how to value the differences that our cultures possess inherently make us better leaders."

Michael Milligan
Board director, Axis Capital Holding and Portland General Electric
Former president, Verizon Global Wholesale

"In today's globally interconnected, complex, and diverse business world, cultural intelligence is a must-have for business leaders and is key to being able to build inclusive, highly engaged, and effective teams."

Rustom Jilla
SVP, CFO
SI Group

"In this book, Tony Lopez unlocks the vault on creating positive, enduring, and real change in how leaders and boards of directors must think about diversity, and how they can become culturally intelligent to fully leverage DE&I strategically and competitively up and down their organizations to drive impressive business results."

Esther Aguilera
President and CEO
Latino Corporate Directors Association (LCDA)

"Tony has taken us full circle on the leadership journey with his latest book on cultural intelligence. As always, he is provocative in his thinking and also fun to read. His message will inspire you to become the best you and will force a better leader to emerge from within."

Monica Diaz
Human Resources, Diversity, Equity & Inclusion executive
Author of *From INTENT to IMPACT: The 5 Dualities of Diversity and Inclusion*

"I have known Tony for many years and when Tony speaks, people need to listen. This book is insightful, and it is right on point, especially in today's world. Understanding cultural intelligence (CQ) is paramount to any business leader of an organization, at all levels, including the board of directors. An organization that does not embrace Diversity, Equity, and Inclusion (DE&I) will not survive. DE&I and CQ is no longer a "nice to have" but an imperative."

Jose R. Rodriguez, partner (retired), KPMG LLP
Independent director, Popular, Inc., Primoris Services Corp., and CareMax, Inc.

"Whether you lead in a small company or a large one, regardless of your industry or sector, and no matter what your personal background is, this book will make you a better leader. Cultural intelligence will become a standard by which we will measure leaders, just as we do with emotional intelligence. In this thought-provoking book, my friend Tony Lopez will get you started on your CQ journey."

Billy Dexter
Managing partner
Heidrick & Struggles

"CQ: The Legacy Leader's Superpower is an exceptional guide for corporate boards on cultural intelligence and their role in organizational culture oversight. Tony does an amazing job outlining the problem and providing clear, tangible guidance to help corporate boards fulfill their fiduciary

duties by providing effective questioning and measurable outcomes to help support leadership teams, ultimately ensuring shareholder value."

Rochelle Campbell
CEO, Leadership Elevated
Board advisor and consultant

CONTENTS

FOREWORD

At a very young age, I had a passion for business and languages. I knew I wanted to work in different parts of the globe. That is what drove my focus on business and languages in college. Growing up in Queens, New York, in a predominantly white neighborhood while only speaking Spanish at home, I understood at a very young age the importance of adapting to your surroundings while never forgetting where you come from. I learned that to be successful, it was necessary not just to be surrounded with people from all different backgrounds, experiences, skill sets, and interests, but to learn how to effectively work with them and, more importantly, to learn from them. Fortunately for me, even in college, I was exposed to people with different interest and backgrounds. My college roommates included an education major, a theatre major, and students with academic pursuits different from my own. I really enjoyed that variety around me then and still enjoy working and collaborating in a diverse environment today.

Once I began my corporate career, two things became painfully clear to me. First, my instinct that understanding cultural and other differences among people, and effectively working with them, was indeed critical to success. Second, that the corporate environment had a long way to go in learning how to welcome, appreciate, and leverage diversity to drive organizational results. Considering that it was the early 1990s, and that "diversity and inclusion" was a very early concept in the corporate setting back then, in hindsight, that conclusion should not be surprising. In retrospect, that is in part why I was motivated to become an early champion of diversity in the workplace and why I was drawn to be actively involved with organizations such as the Association of Latino Professionals For Advancement (ALPFA) and Milagros Para Niños (Miracles for Children), a group I cofounded at Boston Children's Hospital in 2009 to raise funds to support the medical needs of underserved Latino children.

As my career progressed, I was very fortunate to have the opportunity to serve in a number of roles that increasingly exposed me to the global marketplace. I was blessed to have the opportunity to work and live in China, Hong Kong, London, Paris, and many other places. These experiences shaped my thinking and clearly informed my decisions. They helped me to become increasingly successful as my team and I worked with asset managers, asset owners, and insurance companies, helping them define their future state-operating model to enable them to innovate, transform, and make the right investment decisions, all in the context of diverse market conditions and cultural settings. I have no doubt that my understanding of diversity and my own cultural intelligence, were (and are) key enabling leadership traits that have greatly contributed to my success, both personally and professionally. I have come to believe that we must do more to understand how we develop and nurture organizational cultures where leaders can become increasingly global and inclusive in their thinking. Leaders, after all, set the tone for the rest.

In 2017, the National Association of Corporate Directors (NACD) published a report of its Blue-Ribbon Commission entitled "Culture as a Corporate Asset."[1] This three-part report sets out the commission's view on a definition for organizational culture and outlines its key characteristics as well as the factors that are driving a significant change on how boards of directors are engaging with organizational culture and how they conduct oversight. The report goes on to describe culture as a "unifying force" for a company. It states that "culture is revealed through the behaviors of employees at all levels and that if values are the "what" and "why" of an organization, then culture is the "how": the way those values are lived on a day-to-day basis. Moreover, it goes on to describe culture as "reaching beyond the company since it is expressed not only in the treatment of employees, but also in interactions with customers, suppliers, communities, and other external stakeholders." This publication by the NACD even provides a road map, recommendations, and a number of resources for boards to measure organizational culture, its effectiveness, and especially the CEO's role in fostering and enabling the right culture to drive the expected results. Culture is that important to an organization. It therefore makes sense that leaders need to be very adept at understanding culture and their role in building it.

Every employee or member of a team plays an important part in creating organizational culture. However, in the end, it is the leaders who set the tone and, through their actions, cause the culture to evolve. Their actions cause an effect not just in what the company does, but how it goes about doing it. The leader's action has a ripple effect on all aspects of the organization and, most importantly, on employee engagement and the teams' performance. Leaders must consistently demonstrate the beliefs and the values of the company, above all others. They truly must talk the talk and walk the walk. Leaders and organizational culture are mirror images of one another. Organizational culture flows from leaders because they control the resources, people, and processes needed to build or change culture. It's the leaders who motivate and inspire people. Leaders build teams and set the tone of communications in the organization. They set the example and model the behaviors that determine culture.

Thus, given the importance of organizational culture, and the overwhelming role leaders play in building culture, it raises the question, what are the fundamental traits leaders must possess to do that effectively? The answer to that question is, many. Chief among them, however, is that they possess a high level of cultural intelligence (CQ). In this book, my friend Tony Lopez sets forth the Legacy Leader's Cultural Intelligence Accelerator Model, aimed at helping leaders move up the CQ spectrum, use their skills as a culturally intelligent leaders to create high-CQ organizations, and achieve breakthrough results with their teams. In this thoughtful, methodical, and simple-to-read book, Tony essentially provides us a great road map to enable our personal journeys to higher levels of cultural intelligence. Thanks to the insights laid out in the text, I have come to understand the power of CQ and see how it serves as a solid foundation for creating organizations that think in organically diverse ways and deliver outstanding results.

Nearly three decades ago, Daniel Goldman introduced emotional intelligence (EQ) into the corporate psyche. That transformed how we think of leadership. We learned what it meant to be emotionally intelligent and how to develop a higher level of EQ. Since then, having high-EQ leaders has become a part of our normal corporate culture. We measure leaders and professionals by their level of EQ. We have come to expect it as a fundamental trait in successful leaders. We recruit for it, and we counsel individuals when they don't demonstrate a healthy level of emotional intelligence in the workplace. It's that important. Cultural intelligence (CQ) is equally as important as EQ, and perhaps even more so. And what Goldman did for EQ all those years ago, Tony Lopez now does for all of us in this book on CQ. He introduces us to cultural intelligence and helps us understand how we go about developing leadership and organizational CQ. Importantly, Tony also explores the roles of the board and executive leadership teams (ELTs) in enabling and measuring CQ. Consider this book a guide, a road map, if you will, but don't think of it as a recipe. Our personal CQ journeys are as individual as our fingerprints. The good news is this: CQ can be developed, improved, and used effectively; it can be powerful. I challenge all of us to embark on this journey and become high CQ leaders. Our teams, communities, and our families deserve nothing less.

Yvonne Garcia
Global Head of Internal Communications,
Chief of Staff to Chairman and CEO
State Street Corporation

INTRODUCTION

The local time was 12:30 p.m. I was still a bit groggy from the long flight and was preparing to land: stowing my computer, putting my seat in the upright position, and making sure I didn't leave anything behind in the seat pocket in front of me. No sooner we touched down, and as the jet made its way to the gate, the chatty flight attendant was back on the microphone, welcoming us to Kuala Lumpur. I didn't pay too much attention to what she was saying as I looked out the window, but I did hear her say the temperature was 33 degrees Celsius. I was tempted to open my phone app to do the conversion to Fahrenheit but decided that my mental calculation would be close enough. "That's more than 90 degrees," I said to myself, but just loud enough that the person sitting to my left heard me.

"More like 92 or 93," she said, much to both of our chagrin.

I did not need a thermometer to confirm the temperature once I left the terminal. It was hot. I was escorted to a waiting company car, where the friendliest of drivers immediately handed me a cool towel and a bottle of cold water as I settled in the back seat.

"Welcome to KL," he said in good English, albeit it with a local accent. "We have about a ninety, nine-zero, minutes to drive to Melaka and your hotel." I was glad he clarified the nine-zero, because at first, I thought I heard him say nineteen minutes. I was impressed that he knew to clarify the "ninety" with "nine zero," as he was no doubt aware that his accent may have made it hard for me to understand him. He was only partially correct. Over the years, I have learned to listen past accents as much as possible.

"Thank you," I responded, although I must admit I was somewhat annoyed that the drive would be that long.

"This is your first time to Malaysia?" he asked as he pulled away from the curb, looking at me in his rearview mirror.

"No. I've been to KL before. But never to Melaka," I said.

"Oh. It's very different in Melaka from Kuala Lumpur. I think you will like it."

I smiled and nodded. *We'll see*, I thought to myself and settled in for the long ride.

For the next nearly two hours (traffic was worse than the driver had expected), my new friend and I chatted about his hometown of Melaka. He was equally curious about my home island of Puerto Rico and the United States. I learned much from him, and it did make the time pass much quicker.

"Here we are," he said, finally pulling up to the front entrance of the hotel where I was going to spend the next few nights. I was soon escorted to my room and given a quick tutorial on its features by the friendly attendant, who had insisted on pulling my small carry-on suitcase all the way there. As he was ready to exit the room, he said, "Please let us know if there is anything we can do to help you, Mr. Tony. Enjoy your stay."

"Thank you," I said, as I reached for my wallet and quickly pulled out some money to give him a tip. Before I could reach out my hand with the cash, he motioned with his hand and said, "That is not necessary, Mr. Tony, thank you. Have a good afternoon."

Before I could insist, he had smiled and quickly disappeared behind the closing door. I must say I was pleasantly surprised that he had turned down my tip. Coming from the United States, where it seems everyone expects a tip for doing almost anything, it was nice to get good customer service as a standard, with no strings attached. My next thought, however, I will admit, was one of suspicion. *He probably expects a bigger tip at the end of my stay,* I thought to myself. I would come to find out that I was wrong.

It was now just over 3:30 p.m., and I was wide awake, despite the jet lag. I decided to go for a run, even though the temperature was still a balmy and very humid 89 degrees Fahrenheit. As I jogged around the hotel grounds, it wasn't long before I was dripping sweat, and slowing to no faster than a fast walk. As I squinted through my sunglasses, I saw a couple walking in my direction. The closer I got to them, I found myself becoming increasingly annoyed and bothered. Soon I could see them very clearly. The woman was dressed in a black burqa. The man, who I presumed was her husband, was wearing khaki shorts, a shirt straight from the Tommy Bahama collection, flip-flops, and very stylish Ray Bans.

As I walked past them, I nodded and said, "Good afternoon."

They said nothing, although the man did nod back. Making my way back to my room, I found myself going from being annoyed to being angry. *How unfair,* I thought to myself. *Why is the guy able to be in beach attire while the woman bakes in the heat under that black garment?*

By now in the story, you may be having one of a few reactions. First, you may be feeling like I did at that moment. You may be thinking that is unfair. Perhaps you are wondering, as I did, "Why should she have to wear that hot dress when it's 90 degrees out?" Or you may be thinking, *You don't understand, Lopez. Wearing the burka is a choice the woman makes, and it has deep meaning for her.* Maybe you're in between and thinking, *Hey, to each their own. Who am I to judge what someone else does according to their traditions or religion?*

Irrespective of which one of these mindsets best represents your thinking, one thing is certain: Keeping an open mind, suspending judgment, and staying intellectually curious to learn about other's traditions and ways is the beginning of the journey of enlightenment. When you combine broad-mindedness with some information and education, it leads to insight. Putting that insight to work to effectively interact with others is what we call cultural intelligence.

Over the years since that brief encounter on that hot afternoon in Melaka, I have had the privilege of working with many wonderful people in Malaysia and other parts of that region of the world where burkas and other such attire for women is common. I learned that a burka is an article of clothing worn as an outermost layer by women of certain Islamic traditions and that they have become highly politicized items of clothing from many standpoints within the Muslim community. Opponents of this tradition claim that burkas are oppressive to women. They are often in favor of banning them, particularly for young women in school. There are many testimonies of Muslim women who assert that they are not oppressed and that they choose to wear burkas. However, it is also true that in some countries of Islamic tradition, such as areas in Afghanistan and Pakistan, women have been compelled by certain groups to wear full burkas in the face of severe penalties; that seems wrong on every level to me. Clearly there are divergent perspectives on the practice, its meaning, and its impact on women. I would be making a mistake if I painted all with the same brush and assumed to have the right answer in every scenario.

If my story above has elicited an emotional response from you, that was the intent. Sometimes being provocative is a good way to turbocharge a conversation. What I am not trying to make is a statement on Islam or any other religion. Nor am I trying to make a statement about whether women wearing burkas is right or wrong. After all, who am I to say? So, what's my point? Simply this: I had an opinion and a feeling when I first walked past that couple at the hotel. It caused me to think, and likely act, in a certain way. However, I now have a more informed view and position. Although I may still feel a certain way about it and may even believe in my way of thinking that it is wrong, I have learned to suspend my judgment and consider the circumstances before coming to any conclusions or taking actions. That is the nature of cultural intelligence. It allows us to be more insightful in how we respond to situations and people, and generally makes us more effective as we interact with others. We often do this irrespective of how we may feel or without having to betray our own values and beliefs.

My first book on leadership was titled *The Legacy Leader: Leadership with a Purpose*. It was first released in 2003, nearly twenty years ago. As I began to write this latest book, I found myself going back and looking at the first one. Other than the picture of the author, a younger man nearly unrecognizable to me now, I concluded that the concepts, the leadership principles I outlined all those years ago, certainly still ring true and relevant today. That's not surprising since there is likely nothing really new that has been written about leadership since Sun Tzu wrote *The Art of War* more than three thousand years ago. Second perhaps only to the Bible, more books have been written about leadership than almost any other topic. That fact did not sway me from writing several more in what I have come to regard as the *Legacy Leader Series of Books*.

In the series, I captured what I believe is the fundamental cycle of leadership. The journey we travel on our way to becoming increasingly effective leaders, in my view, encompasses the following: First, a leadership philosophy grounded on character and integrity as the fundamental compass of how we behave as leaders. Next, what I refer to as the mechanics of leadership. That is, what we do and how we do it. This is followed by keeping in mind these principles and mechanics as we progress in our careers and also doing critical self-assessments along the way. Finally, as leaders, if we keep in mind the most fundamental traits of inspirational and motivational leadership, we can drive teams to achieve breakthrough results and achieve the status of LegacyWoman or LegacyMan. That is what motivated my books, *The Legacy Leader: Leadership with a Purpose*, *Breakthrough Thinking: The Leader's Role in Driving Innovation*, *The Leader's Lobotomy: The Legacy Leader Avoids Promotion-Induced Amnesia*, *The Leader in the Mirror: The Legacy Leader's Critical Self-Assessment*, and *LEGACYWOMAN: The Legacy Leader as SuperHero*.

The cycle seemed complete with these books. First, you learn to lead with character and integrity as fundamentals, along with learning other mechanical skills. Next, you apply these skills to drive results and breakthrough teams, and you ensure not to forget the lessons along the way. Follow this by evaluating yourself often to learn from your mistakes and make course corrections in your leadership. Finally, you exhibit the traits of the best leaders to become a superhero leader. What could be missing? The answer to that question is this: what is missing is a key anchoring skill that underpins our effectiveness as leaders. That skill is cultural intelligence.

Twenty years ago, I ended the preface of the book with these words:

> I hope this short book will serve as a reminder to some that as leaders, we, more than anyone else, can make a difference; that our leadership must have a fundamentally good purpose. We must labor to create a legacy we can be proud of.

A lifetime later, these words still ring true to me. I have had the privilege to serve in a number of executive leadership roles with thousands of people in global organizations with overall business accountability. I grew up in Puerto Rico and have been blessed to live in many different places and even a few different countries. I have been incredibly fortunate to have the opportunity to travel across the globe and have worked extensively with people from every region of the world. Those experiences, and the gray hairs that came along with them, have shaped me personally and professionally. I can say confidently, albeit humbly, that there is now no doubt that being a culturally intelligent leader has been one of the key factors in whatever level of success I have enjoyed as a leader.

This book's primary intent is to help leaders understand cultural intelligence and enable their personal journey to become high-CQ individuals, thereby fueling their effectiveness as leaders. We will also explore how leaders can influence and drive organizations to strengthen its cultural intelligence. Lastly, we will dive into how boards and leadership teams can model and measure CQ as an enabler of results in the companies they lead.

The book is structured in four parts. In Part 1, we will fully define cultural intelligence and why it's critical to leaders and the organizations they lead. We'll dedicate Part 2 to exploring how we go about developing leadership and organizational CQ. Part 3 will explore how we enable CQ up and down the organization to create an organically diverse-thinking organization. In Part 4, we will outline the board's and executive teams' role in enabling and measuring CQ. Throughout the book, I'll use anecdotes to illustrate the points. These stories, and the lessons we draw from them, are all based on actual events. Finally, I trust this book will challenge you to embark on your personal journey to achieving higher levels of CQ and to reach your full potential as a leader.

PART 1

CQ: What Is It and Why Is It Important?

CHAPTER 1

Cultural Intelligence (CQ): A Key Leadership Trait

For more than thirty years, I have been a student and a practitioner of leadership. No doubt, leadership, leaders, and their impact on all aspects of human history has been one of the most written about and studied subjects of all time. My small contribution to the body of work as it relates to the study of the art of leadership is captured in the *Legacy Leader* series of books. In the books, I outline what I believe can be best described as the journey leaders walk through during the course of their career as they impact and influence the people they are privileged to lead. I begin and end with the thesis that the purpose of a leader is to create a legacy that others will be proud of when they are gone. That in doing so, they would have led with character and integrity and with a noble purpose that created value for the world around them. The paths to achieve this purpose are many. The leadership styles and approaches leaders take as they lead are as diverse as the industries or sectors they operate in. In fact, these differences are influenced by where and when leaders lead. Whether it's the private or public sector, military or government service, religious or academic institutions, local or international, large or small businesses, leaders come in many packages and rise to their positions for many reasons.

Martin Luther King Jr. was the right leader at the right time to spark the civil rights movement in the United States in the 1960s. Winston Churchill led the United Kingdom through some of its darkest history during World War II. Barack Obama sparked the imagination of a younger generation of Americans and caused an awakening in moving them to become more civically minded. Robert Burke led Johnson & Johnson through the famous Tylenol issue back in the 1980s that still today is held as an ethical and CREDO-based way of behaving. Rosa Parks will forever be remembered in history for refusing to give up her seat on a racially segregated bus, leading to the Montgomery bus boycott. After the boycott helped end segregation in public spaces, Mrs. Parks sought to educate the nation's youth about civil rights. Perhaps she never set out to lead, but her actions propelled her into a leadership role, and she rose to the challenge and became an inspiration to millions in the process. We can go on with example after example of legacy leaders and the impact they have had in human history. Leaders are diverse in their personalities, styles, and approaches, as are the circumstances in which they lead.

Trying to bottle a formula for great leadership would be futile. However, understanding the most significant traits leaders must embody to effectively inspire, motivate, and lead people is of great value. There is room for debate on what the essential traits are that can be learned and practiced, to build the muscle memory that enables leaders to effectively lead. In my most recent book, *LEGACYWOMAN: The Legacy Leader as SuperHero*, I outline what I believe these most essential traits are. In summary, these are some of the traits:

- o   visionary and ethical
- o   truthful and credible
- o   loyal
- o   courageous
- o   innovative and breakthrough thinking

- o emotionally and culturally intelligent
- o adaptable
- o flexible
- o transparent
- o passionate

Each of these traits, properly leveraged, significantly increases a leader's ability to influence a positive and consistent outcome. Leaders who are visionary, ethical, and truthful gain credibility. If they courageously leverage that credibility to drive innovative thinking by their followers and passionately pursue their mission and purpose, the results will follow. If they remain adaptable to changing conditions, flex their style and strategy, and communicate transparently and honestly with their followers, the inevitable outcome will be success. Here's the catch: it takes an emotionally and culturally intelligent leader to be able to demonstrate these soft skills.

If we are to understand cultural intelligence, we need to start with a broader understanding of intelligence. To start, I did a Google search with the phrase "different forms of intelligence." In a few milliseconds, I had access to 666,000,000 search hits. Suffice it to say that defining intelligence is a rather complicated task. However, when we hear the word *intelligence*, most of us think first of the concept of IQ. So let's start there.

Intelligence is often defined as our intellectual potential. It is considered something we are born with, that can be measured, and that is difficult to change. In other words, if you weren't born to be Einstein, you probably will never become Einstein-like in your level of IQ. Fortunately for me, and for most of us, that's not a problem. Just having an average level of IQ works just fine, thank you.

In recent years, other views about how to define intelligence have emerged. One such idea was put forward by Harvard psychologist Howard Gardner.

He first outlined his theory of multiple intelligences in his 1983 book *Frames of Mind: The Theory of Multiple Intelligences*.[2] Specifically, he defines eight intelligences and even has suggested a ninth, known as "existentialist intelligence." If you are a psych major, you are probably having flashbacks to your college days and philosophical discussions with your professor about the validity of Gardner's theory. It certainly has been debated by academics since it was first introduced. Critics argue that his definition of intelligence is too broad and includes talents, personality traits, and abilities. Suffice it to say that intelligence is harder to define than we might think. However, it's not that hard to see. We all know people who we consider smart. We also know many who maybe received a bit less in the gray matter allocation. Whatever definition we want to use, we can probably all agree that, as was suggested in the definition above, while we can learn to be smarter (read "more intelligent"), we are always going to be somewhat limited in transforming our IQ level. Moreover, through a series of standardized tests, we can each be assigned an IQ number, with the vast majority of the population landing somewhere between 85 and 115. If you are curious, Einstein's IQ was estimated between 160 and 180.

Relative to our discussion on leadership, a good question may be, how is IQ level related to the effectiveness of a leader? The answer may not surprise you that much. When you ask people about what they think the important qualities of a good leader are, you get a plethora of answers. Most, however, mention things such as having vision, people skills, and integrity. They also mention intelligence as a desirable trait. However, some new research conducted by Switzerland's University of Lausanne and published in the *Journal of Applied Psychology* suggest that having a very high IQ is not necessarily such a good thing when it comes to leadership. It turns out that the brightest people are actually less effective as leaders. The study showed that the average IQ level for leaders was 111, or about 11 points higher than the average for the general population. Moreover, through additional testing, the researchers studied how the leader demonstrated various leadership styles such as transformational, instrumental, or passive. While they noted variances based on age and sex, they concluded that the majority of the variance came from personality and intelligence.

It turns out, according to the study, when the leaders' IQ scores rose to 128 or above, the association with less effective leadership methods are clear and statistically significant. The reasons are not as simple to pinpoint. It may be that highly intelligent people are sometimes unable to effectively communicate clearly enough or explain complex tasks. Perhaps their minds work at speeds that make it harder for them to understand why others struggle with a problem they find simple. It may be that they find it harder to be seen as relatable or approachable. My conclusion is that this is good news for many of us. As was already suggested, an average level of intelligence is more than good enough as one of the leader's necessary traits.

A second form of intelligence that has become a part of our normal vernacular is emotional intelligence (EQ). In Gardner's theory of multiple intelligences, the intelligences he defines that most closely embody what we think of as EQ are interpersonal and intrapersonal intelligence. The other seven intelligences in his theory are visual-spatial, linguistic-verbal, logical-mathematical, musical, bodily-kinesthetic, naturalistic, and existential.

Emotional intelligence has been studied and written about for many years. It's a term that was created by two researchers, Peter Salavoy and John Mayer. It gained popularity thanks to Dan Goleman's 1996 book *Emotional Intelligence*.[3] Now there are countless books, articles, and workshops to help us all understand the concept of EQ and apply it to our daily lives. Basically, EQ is defined as the ability to recognize, understand, and manage our emotions and recognize, understand, and influence the emotions of others. Having a high EQ is a very important leadership trait, as it means being aware that emotions can drive our behavior and influence people. Thus, learning how to manage those emotions, especially when under pressure, is a key strength of a leader.

Goleman references five components of EQ:

- o Self-awareness: This implies that you can see your own patterns of behaviors and motives. You understand how your emotions and actions affect those around you, and importantly, you recognize your triggers.
- o Self-regulation: This means that you can manage your emotional reactions according to the given situation or circumstances. It suggests that you know how to control your impulses and your responses. You think before you act, and you are adept at managing conflict and coping with tough situations.
- o Motivation: Being motivated means you have an interest in your personal development. You're highly driven to succeed, and you are goal driven by your growth more so than rewards such as fame, money, or even recognition.
- o Empathy: This refers to your ability to connect emotionally with others. It implies that while you have a healthy level of self-interest, you are not self-centered. You put yourself in the other person's position and try to see things from their point of view, and you are able to draw from your own personal experiences to connect with people rather than to judge them.
- o Social skills: This may be the easiest to define. Simply put, you have a healthy and well-developed ability to interact socially. You are considerate of others and their needs in conversations. People generally view you as welcoming and a good listener, with a comfortable style and easy-going body language to go along with excellent communications skills. We might say, you build rapport and are generally well-liked.

Read those five descriptors one more time. It's not hard to see why having a high level of EQ is critical for a leader. Some leaders are self-aware, can regulate their behavior, can demonstrate a high level of empathy and social skills, and are motivated to continuously improve themselves; that sound like someone I want to follow. It's not easy to be good at all of those all the time. Like IQ, we can measure ourselves and see where we are in our level of EQ. The good news is that unlike IQ, with some work, we have a very good shot at improving our EQ levels. The best news is this: Having a high EQ level is immensely more important than having a high IQ level. The data are very clear that high EQ leaders are better leaders and achieve greater long-term results.

While IQ and EQ have been studied and written about longer, cultural intelligence or cultural quotient (CQ) is a more recent concept. It's a term used in business, education, government, and academic research. As the words imply, CQ is the capability to relate and work effectively across cultures. Early studies of the concepts were published by P. Christopher Earley and Soon Ang in the book *Cultural Intelligence: Individual Interactions across Cultures* (2003).[4] Later, in his book *Leading with Cultural Intelligence*,[5] David Livermore developed the idea fully. The concept focuses on cross-cultural competence but goes beyond that to consider intercultural capabilities as a form of intelligence that can be measured and developed. Earley and Ang defined CQ as "a person's capability to adapt as she or he interacts with others from different cultural regions, and has behavioral, motivational, and metacognitive aspects." Later, in chapter 3, we will discuss the dimensions of cultural intelligences as described by Livermore, Early, Ang, and others. Having this academic understanding is helpful to charting our personal journeys to cultural intelligence.

CQ is measured on a scale similar to that used to measure an intelligence quotient (IQ). People with higher CQs are regarded as better able to successfully blend into any environment, using more effective business practices, than those with a lower CQ. There are now a number of academically validated assessments (such as the one created by Ang and Linn Van Dyne) being used to assess an individual's CQ level. There are also a number of centers conducting research and other work on CQ, such as the Cultural Intelligence Center in the United States. The research suggests that CQ is consistent predictor of performance in multicultural settings. A simple google search on CQ yields volumes of great information, most of it hovering around the same idea. I have found, however, that in Christopher Earley's and Elaine Mosakowski's *Harvard Business Review* article published in the October 2004 issue, they provide a perspective on cultural intelligence that best embodies why it's important for a leader to have a high level of CQ. In their article, they write:

> You see them at international airports like Heathrow: posters advertising the global bank HSBC that show a grasshopper and the message "USA—Pest. China—Pet. Northern Thailand—Appetizer." Taxonomists pinned down the scientific definition of the family Acrididae more than two centuries ago. But culture is so powerful it can affect how even a lowly insect is perceived. So, it should come as no surprise that the human actions, gestures, and speech patterns a person encounters in a foreign business setting are subject to an even wider range of interpretations, including ones that can make misunderstandings likely and cooperation impossible. But occasionally an outsider has a seemingly natural ability to interpret someone's unfamiliar and ambiguous gestures in just the way that person's compatriots and colleagues would, even to mirror them. We call that cultural intelligence or CQ. In a world where crossing boundaries is routine, CQ becomes a vitally important aptitude and skill, and not just for international bankers and borrowers."

That definition resonated with me. Throughout my career, I have had the opportunity to travel extensively to countries throughout the world. As president of Ansell Healthcare, of the more than four thousand people in my organization, 80 percent were not from the United States, where the company was based, but rather they were from countries on every continent, living and working in every region of the world. Our primary manufacturing plants were in Malaysia, Sri Lanka, and Mexico. Our customers operated in almost every country on the globe. More often than not, I found myself in a foreign country, meeting with customers, business partners, healthcare providers, not to mention my employees. I enjoyed the opportunity to experience first-hand cultures and customs as varied as the countries themselves, from New Zealand, China, and Japan, to east and west European nations, to South Africa, and everything in between. Meetings were often conducted through translators, in remote areas of India and China, for instance. Fortunately for me, I enjoyed it tremendously. I was often in awe as I experienced cultural events, tasted the local foods, and learned new customs and traditions on how the business world operated in these countries. The lessons were constant and invaluable, and helped me develop as a global leader. I found that allowing myself to be integrated as much as possible into the moment, participating when offered the chance in some ritual, tradition, or event, and being conspicuously intellectually curious about the surroundings, not only added to my learnings, but immediately made my hosts and all around me feel a genuine like for me, perhaps even a respect. It was a rather constant reminder of the importance of CQ to be an effective leader.

In this author's view, CQ is an imperative trait for great leadership. It's not optional or a nice to have. It's a must. We live and work in a diverse and complex world that has been made smaller with technology. Unless you are living and working in remote areas, there is a high probability that you are interacting and trying to influence outcomes with people from different backgrounds, beliefs, practices, and many more elements of diversity, seen and unseen. This skill is so important for leaders personally, and for their teams collectively, that we will dedicate the balance of this book to diving deeply into what it is, how to develop it, how to apply it, and how to measure it. I trust these first few pages have enticed you to embark on the CQ journey with me.

During a recent presentation I was delivering, I was asked if there was a recipe for CQ. I've already mentioned there is no such thing; however, in that moment, the only thought that came to my mind was to say, "A recipe for great leaders is three teaspoons of IQ, four tablespoons of EQ, and two cups of CQ." My obvious point being to suggest the relative importance of the three. In all of my books, I have insisted that our goal should be to become a Legacy Leader. Well, you can't be one unless you are also a high-CQ leader. Let's go.

CHAPTER 2

The Impact of Culture on Organizational Culture and the Need for CQ

Defining Culture and Organizational Culture

Read the title of this first subsection of the chapter one more time: "Defining Culture and Organizational Culture." Aren't they the same thing? Clearly, they are not. For our purposes, as we begin to study cultural intelligence, the word *culture* in that context refers specifically to its academic definition. It refers to the customs, art, social institutions, and achievements of a particular people, nation, or other social group. It is manifested in how that group collectively generally behaves, how they think, and what they believe. While it would be a mistake to make assumptions that these behaviors, ideas, and beliefs are held uniformly by every member of that group (i.e., stereotypes), it provides those of us not in that group a point of reference, perhaps even a bias, about them. Although it is impossible to tell exactly how many cultures there are in the world, many academics use language as an indicator. There are between five thousand and six thousand languages in the world, give or take a syllable or two. We can therefore agree that we have diversity in cultures.

It is this definition of culture that we are referencing when talking about diversity in the workplace. We will explore the relationship between CQ and Diversity, Equity, and Inclusion (DE&I) later in the book. For now, suffice it to say that CQ does not replace the need for solid diversity, equity, and inclusion strategies in organizations. Instead, CQ enables DE&I to happen in a more organic way through all levels of the organization. So what, then, is the relationship between culture and organizational culture? Let's answer that question by first defining what we really mean by organizational culture. If this seems like circular reasoning, hang in there with me just a bit longer, and we'll connect the dots.

How often have you been asked about the organizational culture in your company? It's a standard question at many networking encounters and business conferences. It's a guaranteed question to be asked during a job interview, either by the interviewer or the interviewee. However, let's pause for a moment and answer this question: What is organizational culture? These words may have lost some of their meaning with overuse or, perhaps, as a result of being misused. I would be willing to lay down some odds that if you take three people in a company and ask them that simple question, you will get three different answers. Some may articulate the stated values of the company and say they have a culture driven and measured by those values. Others may talk about how they perceive the environment in the company, using words like friendly, high energy, laid-back, challenging, motivating, or stressful. Yet others may describe it in terms of style and use contemporary words reflective of latest trends in music, fashion, politics, or other social trends. There can be little doubt that how a millennial employee describes the culture of the organization as compared to how a Generation X (let alone a baby boomer) expresses it are going to be dramatically different. Is it any surprise, then, that so few organizations really understand what their true organizational culture is? Not what they say it is, but what it really is.

Sadly, organizational culture is usually taken for granted until there is a problem whose root cause is determined to have more to do with how people are working together, rather than what they are working on. Managers and leaders scratch their heads and wonder why people are not collaborating effectively or why there seems to be such lack of alignment on the objectives. They can't understand why people seem unmotivated or unwilling to take the initiative, let alone their willingness to take prudent risks. They call management meetings and ask, with a clear hint of frustration in their voice, "Where's the accountability with our people?" Before long, someone in the meeting says, "We need to change the culture around here." The harsh reality is that before the leaders can ever hope to have a shot at affecting organizational culture, they need to first understand what it truly means, how it's created, what the drivers are, and how to influence it.

Culture and organizational culture both have many dimensions to them. We already estimated the number of cultures in the thousands. Fortunately, most experts have categorized organizational culture in a few types, each with a number of descriptors. The culture of the people within that organization is but one (albeit it a very important) element that ultimately defines the organizational culture. This is because the simplest and my favorite definition of organizational culture is "the way we do things around here." If we can articulate the way a team goes about its daily work, then we are describing the organizational culture. It is evident in the shared beliefs, values, and norms held by team members. Notice the emphasis on the word "shared." You see, each culture has its own set of beliefs, values, and norms, and since our teams are made up of these diverse individuals, they will likely all have their own way of thinking about it. What defines the organizational culture is the resulting aggregation of all these divergent points of view and the resulting shared ways of thinking and acting. Therein lies not just the key to creating great organizational cultures, but the power and effectiveness of that culture.

The best leaders, the culturally intelligent ones, understand this. They fundamentally understand that they must harness the individual strengths of the diverse cultures represented by the people in their team and align them with a shared set of values to achieve a mutually beneficial objective.

The Leader's Role in Organizational Culture

There have been many different models set forth to help organizations understand organizational culture. One model describes six types of organizational culture: empowered culture, culture of innovation, sales culture, customer-centric culture, a culture of leadership excellence, and a culture of safety. Another better-known model was introduced by Kim Cameron and Robert Quinn from the University of Michigan. They define four types of organizational culture: Clan, Adhocracy, Market, and Hierarchy. According to their theory, every organization has its own particular combination. A third model defines organizational culture by styles of how the organization behaves. This model refers to seven specific styles to describe the organizational culture: innovative, aggressive, outcome-oriented, stable, people-oriented, team-oriented, and detailed-oriented.

It's not my intention in this work to describe these in any further detail or argue one being better than the other. They all have essentially valid ways of describing what we already stated organizational culture to be. Again, organizational culture is visible in the way work gets done daily. It is evident in the behaviors of individuals and groups. Whatever model we choose to describe it, our goal should be to clearly articulate two things: first, how things are done now and what we value most in how people behave. Second, and more importantly, how we want things to be done and how we want people to behave going forward. Only then can we chart a path to enable us to create the culture we want in our organizations.

In the 2017 NACD Blue Ribbon Commission on Culture as a Corporate Asset,[1] the authors concluded that

> the board, the CEO, and the senior management need to establish clarity on the foundational elements of values and culture—where consistent behavior is expected across the entire organization regardless of geography or operating unit and develop concrete incentives, policies, and controls to support the desired culture.

That is a rather clear statement of the important role leaders play in driving culture. Leaders set the tone in an organization. It is they who establish behavioral standards. They model the values that others will emulate. The best leaders build their teams consistent with those values. They hire and fire based on the values they want to have demonstrated in how work gets done daily. Leaders must communicate relentlessly the values and norms they expect will guide the members of the team from the boardroom to the mailroom. These culturally intelligent leaders don't just embrace diversity or give it lip service. They leverage it to the fullest.

The Need for CQ Leaders

We have all heard the famous quote from the legendary management consultant and writer Peter Drucker that "culture eats strategy for breakfast." If that is true, and I believe it is, then we must keep in mind that culture is the shadow of the leader. Thus, we need strong, culturally intelligent leaders to drive organizations in this complex, multicultural world we live in. The shifting landscape of business opportunities, almost always affected by global macroeconomic trends, demand leaders who can operate well within that environment. The diversity of the markets, customers, and workforces requires leaders who can behave in culturally intelligent ways and seize the advantage it affords them. If these are not reason enough, studies have shown a connection between a high-CQ leader's level of stamina, energy, and productivity and the effectiveness of the teams they lead.

In his book *Leading with Cultural Intelligence,*[5] David Livermore writes:

> Ninety percent of leading executives from sixty-eight countries identified cross-cultural leadership as the top management challenge for the next century. Most contemporary leaders encounter dozens of different cultures daily. It's impossible to master all the norms and values of each culture, but effective leadership does require some adaptation in approach and strategy. The most pressing issues executives identify for why culture intelligence is needed are:

- o Diverse markets
- o Multicultural workforce
- o Attract and retain top talent
- o Profitability and cost savings

The bottom line is that high-CQ leaders

- o are better negotiators and collaborators,
- o are able to build trust more effectively,
- o are good listeners,
- o are more creative and innovative,
- o are more empathetic and often display a higher level of EQ,
- o make better decisions and demonstrate good judgment when working with intercultural issues,
- o are talent magnets,

- ○ are more in tune with market trends affecting results, and
- ○ are able to gain respect quickly.

It's an open-and-shut case: Becoming a high-CQ leader is fundamental to enabling a leader to become an effective driver of breakthrough results in their organizations, and in helping them build legacies they can be proud of.

CHAPTER 3

CQ Capabilities: An Academic Perspective

In this chapter, we will cover the basics of CQ theory from an academic perspective, with some actionable suggestions sprinkled throughout. The work done by experts over the past several decades to advance the understanding of cultural intelligence, some of whom we will quote in this chapter, is very good. Their books and other writings have provided us a strong foundation in the academic, data-driven application of CQ. Although, admittedly, the complexity of a more academic approach can seem a bit dry and even tedious, it is important that we march through it to gain a solid understanding of the concept of CQ. One important point as you read through this chapter is this: It is not my intent to minimize or oversimplify the amazing body of work that so many psychologists and thought leaders have put forward in this field. It is my intent to simply provide a higher level, albeit comprehensive, review and overview of the concept of CQ, how it's defined, and how it can be measured.

While there can be several definitions of CQ, each with its own nuance, here a straight-forward definition that I believe ties it all together: "CQ is the leader's ability to relate to culturally diverse situations (not just people) and work effectively with them. High-CQ leaders are able to better accomplish goals in a respectful way, regardless of the cultural context." As we previously stated, the term CQ is relatively recent, dating back only to the early 2000s. The work done by psychologists Early, Ang, and Livermore set the standard for the academic understanding of CQ. They have written a number of good books, such as *Cultural Intelligence: Individual Interactions Across Cultures*[4] (Eng, Early) and *Leading with Cultural Intelligence*[5] (Livermore), that have helped us grasp the concepts of CQ and understand how to measure it within ourselves and how we can develop higher levels of CQ.

Measuring Our CQ

Some of the most important work done in Cultural intelligence is the academically validated assessment created by Drs. Linn Van Dyne and Soon Ang. The assessment is available from the Culture Intelligence Center based in East Lansing, Michigan. It provides a terrific benchmark and understanding of where we currently stand on the CQ scale, as measured against four defined capabilities: CQ Drive, CQ Knowledge, CQ Strategy, and CQ Action. The assessments go beyond those capabilities and give us a good view of other dimensions of our personality and cultural understanding in a section of the report labeled Cultural Values. Cultural value orientations are based on ten cultural value dimensions. Each of us has personal preferences or individual cultural value orientations. These ten cultural value dimensions are then grouped into cultural clusters that represent the ten largest cultural groupings in the world. Let's describe these further.

In Livermore's book *Leading with Cultural Intelligence (2nd Edition),*[6] he writes:

Cultural values are what get emphasized most when teaching people about cross-cultural leadership. How do people in Mexico approach time or authority compared with people in Germany? Although cultural values are only one dimension of what you need to know to effectively lead with cultural intelligence, they are a significant part of building your repertoire of cultural understanding.

He goes on to point out that all the usual cautions against stereotypes apply to this analysis. Meaning it's dangerous to assume that all people from a culture act a particular way or think similarly. He writes:

As long as we remain open to expecting variability among different people from the same culture (e.g., some Latinos are more concerned about punctuality than others), using cultural norms as a best first guess is worthwhile for shaping initial expectations and interactions.

With that as a basic background, here's how they define the ten value orientations and the associated clusters (with a slight interpretation from this author):

o *Individualism versus Collectivism.* Where is our emphasis? Is it on individual goals and rights, as opposed to the group's goals and personal relationships?

o *Power Distance.* Do we place emphasis on equality and shared decision-making or on difference in status, where superiors make decisions?

o *Uncertainty Avoidance.* Do we emphasize or prefer flexibility and adaptability or planning and predictability?

- o *Cooperative versus Competitive*: Is our emphasis on collaboration, nurturing, and family, or on competition, assertiveness, and getting results?
- o *Short Term versus Long Term*. Do we focus on immediate outcomes or long-term planning?
- o *Direct Context versus Indirect Context*: Is the emphasis on explicit communications or indirect communication?
- o *Being versus Doing*: Are we more concerned about quality of life or being busy and meeting goals?
- o *Universalism versus Particularism*: Are we more comfortable with rules and standards that apply to everyone, or do we prefer unique standards based on relationships?
- o *Neutral versus Affective*: Is our emphasis on non-emotional communication and not being totally transparent with our feelings, or is our emphasis on expressive communication and open sharing of feelings?
- o *Monochromic versus Polychronic*: Is our emphasis on one thing at a time and keeping personal and work life separate, or is the preference towards multitasking and combining work and personal life?

Here are the ten largest cultural groupings, broadly defined (with a few of the countries represented in the group):

- o Anglo: Australia, Canada, New Zealand, USA, UK
- o Arab: Egypt, Jordan, Lebanon, Morocco, Saudi Arabia, U.A.E.
- o Asia: China, Hong Kong, Japan, Singapore, South Korea
- o Eastern Europe: Albania, Greece, Hungary, Mongolia, Poland, Russia
- o Germanic Europe: Austria, Belgium, Germany, Netherlands
- o Latin America: Argentina, Bolivia, Brazil, Chile, Colombia, Costa Rica, Mexico

o   Latin Europe: France, Italy, Portugal, Spain

o   Nordic Europe: Denmark, Finland, Iceland, Norway, Sweden

o   Sub-Saharan Africa: Ghana, Namibia, Nigeria, Zimbabwe

o   Southern Asia: India, Indonesia, Philippines, Malaysia, Thailand

When these cultural values are combined or grouped with the clusters, and our own preferences are mapped as they are in the assessment, the result provides us a clear picture of where we stand relative to other individuals and groups. It provides us a map of how we see things when compared to others. Armed with that knowledge we are certainly in a stronger position to interact effectively across people from different backgrounds and ways of thinking which is indeed the end goal in becoming a high-CQ individual.

CQ is measured on a scale, similar to that used to measure an individual's intelligence quotient. People with higher CQs are regarded as better able to successfully blend into any environment, using more effective business practices, than those with a lower CQ. Published research, sited in peer-reviewed journals, has shown CQ is a consistent predictor of performance in multicultural settings. Having a clear understanding of where we are on our CQ journey is key for several reasons: first, it gives us a starting point. Second, it narrows the focus areas. We may already be naturally strong in some dimensions of CQ and weaker in others. Knowing this helps us to work on a more effective development plan.

Next, let's look at the four CQ capabilities.

Four CQ Capabilities

In 2015, the SHRM Foundation's Effective Practice Guideline Series published *Cultural Intelligence: The Essential Intelligence for the 21ˢᵗ Century.*[7]

In this paper, they describe what researchers at the Cultural Intelligence Center have identified as the four CQ capabilities:

○ *CQ Drive*: This is the motivational dimension of cultural intelligence, measuring the level of interest, drive and energy needed to adapt cross-culturally. If a leader is going to develop a high level of CQ, they must have the courage and stamina to drive through the challenges and conflicts that inevitably accompany intercultural work. Leaders with high-CQ drive are motivated to learn and adapt to new and diverse cultural settings. Their confidence in their adaptive abilities will influence the way they perform in multicultural situations. The level to which we will have a high-CQ drive comes down to this simple question: Just how much do we want to do it? Will we be able to be honest with ourselves and deal with biases that can get in the way of developing CQ? Are we willing to get comfortable with being uncomfortable and spending time in environments that may be strange to us? How willing are we to stay open minded and curious about others? How important do we really believe this is? Tough questions that we must all deal with head-on.

○ *CQ Knowledge*: This is the cognitive dimension of cultural intelligence, referring to knowledge about culture and its role in shaping interactions and work. If CQ Drive is the "Do I want to know?" CQ Knowledge is the "What do I need to know?" Leaders have to work to understand the way culture shapes how people think and how they behave. The more they understand the intercultural norms and differences, the more able they will be to navigate them. The best leaders have a high CQ knowledge and possess sufficient understanding of how other cultures are and what shapes how individuals from that culture think or generally behave. There is no practical way that we can know everything there is to know about all other cultures or groups in the globe, but we certainly have access to a good deal of information that we can learn from. Those most fortunate have the opportunity to experience these cultural differences first-hand because of their travel and work experiences. Whether first-hand or from books, videos, or other materials, we certainly have much we can learn about economic, family, legal, and educational structures, religious practices, and languages of other groups. The more we know, the higher our CQ knowledge. The best leaders understand this simple fact, and they make it a priority to be as educated as they can be about different cultures.

o *CQ Strategy*: This is the metacognitive aspect of cultural intelligence, measuring a person's ability to strategize before, during and after crossing cultures. For a leader, this is a key strength to develop. The primary hurdle is to ensure that we can block our own biases, slow down our thinking enough to suspend judgment, and carefully observe what is going on inside the minds of others. CQ Strategy answers the question "How should I plan for this interaction?" It's our ability to leverage our CQ Drive (our desire to have a good interaction) and our CQ Knowledge (how much we know about who we are interacting with) to build a well-reasoned approach to the interaction. Great leaders have an innate way to use their cultural understanding to develop plans for new intercultural situations, just like they would use any other business information to develop a good action plan. When we work on a business strategy, we analyze data, check our assumptions and environmental conditions, and come up with tactics based on all three of these factors. Developing a good CQ Action plan is no different from this.

o *CQ Action*: This is where the rubber meets the road relative to cultural intelligence. CQ Action is the behavioral dimension of cultural intelligence. It's the leader's ability to act appropriately in a range of multicultural situations to lead the team to effectively accomplish objectives. CQ Action is about "what do I need to do, and what behaviors do I need to adjust for an effective interaction?" It's important that leaders have sound judgment on when and how to act so as to be perceived as in tune with the cultural factors involved. When they can do that effectively, they are seen as adaptive and flexible, both important traits for leaders. Importantly, and as always, the leader's body language speaks volumes and perhaps louder than the actual words used. Therefore, leaders learn to manage their verbal and nonverbal actions appropriately. It is useless to have a high CQ Drive, high CQ Knowledge, and high CQ Strategy, if we don't put it to work via action. Leaders with high-CQ Action leverage the other three capabilities and fearlessly lean into an interaction, confident they are well prepared for a positive exchange.

Putting CQ to Work

In his book, *Leading with Cultural Intelligence,*[5] David Livermore writes:

> Leaders with high CQ Action can draw on the other three capabilities of CQ to translate their enhanced motivation, understanding, and planning into action. They possess a broad repertoire of behaviors, which they can use depending on the context.

What I like most about that quote is that it gets to the point that this is all about action. I also appreciate that he refers to a "repertoire of behaviors," making it clear that CQ Action is a dynamic, evolving, and constantly adjusting process. Here are some ways that leaders can put cultural intelligence into action in practical ways:

- o Hold ourselves to the highest standards relative to expanding our knowledge of other cultures and people's way of thinking and doing things.
- o Stay attentive to learning about the most important practices in different cultures. We don't need to know everything, but we certainly can know a few things.
- o Avoid taboos, generalizations, and assumptions.
- o Ask for feedback relative to how others perceive folks from your background.
- o Learn from the locals. When possible, lean on someone that can help you navigate the cultural norms and traditions.
- o Model behaviors and expect the same from others.
- o Have a zero tolerance for inappropriate behaviors, jokes, or derogatory language.
- o Be well in tune with the communication styles that would work best for a given cultural circumstance. Consider the following:
  - Should you be direct or more subtle?
  - Should you use humor or be straightforward in your approach?
  - How should you deal with compliments and apologies?
  - Understand the preferences of personal space when interacting with different cultures (e.g., how close do people get when speaking?).
  - Be aware of perceptions relative to touching, eye contact, facial expressions, and body language.
- o Understand business practices according to local cultural norms and traditions.
  - When negotiating, what is the goal? Should you focus on the contract or the relationship?
  - How is your personal style perceived by the other party?

- Do they communicate directly in business or more in a roundabout way?
- Are they time sensitive or relationship focused?
- How are agreements indicated? Is a handshake as good as a done deal, or is a more formal agreement needed to seal the deal?
- What is their risk tolerance preference?

Developing these four dimensions for achieving high CQ requires focus and effort. Development plans should identify leaders' current strength level in these areas via an appropriate assessment tool. There are many constructs and instruments available to measure CQ. Some instruments assess an individual's traits and demographic characteristics. This would be similar to what is measured in an Insights, Myers-Briggs, or DISC assessment, but with an emphasis on traits related to intercultural interactions. Other instruments aim at identifying hidden or unconscious biases, many of which develop in our formative early childhood years. These are often the hardest to overcome. Yet other assessments focus on personality, attitudes, beliefs, opinions, and capabilities. The range of tests are as varied as the needs of the leaders taking them. A Human Resources colleague can help make an assessment of the best instruments to use. Whichever ones are chosen, the key, as with any development plan, is to have a realistic and actionable plan to drive real and measurable improvement.

As first mentioned at the outset, the intent of this chapter was to help us understand the basics of CQ theory from the academic perspective and to establish a foundation that will allow us to become individuals with higher CQ levels. The body of work on CQ is as impressive as it is extensive and complex. At times, we can get lost in trying to peel back the multiple layers and dimensions of CQ. Specifically, for leaders, many of whom tend to be rather bottom-line thinkers, a simpler and more actionable approach may be beneficial. This was my primary motivation for developing the

Legacy Leader CQ Acceleration Model that we will present beginning in chapter 4.

Developing higher CQ is a lifelong journey. As we gain experience and challenge our minds to remain open and curious to learn about other cultures and customs, we begin to develop an ability to regulate our own behaviors to better assimilate to the environment around us. This does not mean leaders should abandon their authenticity or behave in ways that are uncomfortable. They should allow themselves to be incorporated into the environment they are currently operating in. To be a true Legacy Leader, you must concern yourself with your CQ index, and you must be committed to the process of continuous improvement to become a high-CQ leader.

PART 2

Developing Leadership
and Organizational CQ

CHAPTER 4

The Legacy Leader CQ Accelerator Model

Chapter 3 explored CQ from a psychological and academic perspective. The work done by many experts, like Soon Ang, Linn Van Dyne, and David Livermore, has informed us on the many dimensions of cultural intelligence. They certainly have the data to support the theories, models, and benchmark testing we now have available to us.

Over the past years, as I embarked on my own personal journey of trying to improve my CQ, it became clear to me that we needed a simpler—and perhaps more actionable—way to enable leaders to accept the challenge of becoming high-CQ leaders. As my thinking on the subject evolved, the idea that it may be as straightforward as a three-step process, became evident. First, I have to know myself, where I come from, and how I show up. Second, as a leader, I must model the right behaviors. Third, I have to find ways to infuse CQ principles into the people and the organizations I influence. When I first wrote this paragraph, I used the word *simple*, and then replaced that word with *straightforward*, in the sentence above. Calling it *simple* would be minimizing the work it takes to be a high CQ individual. It may not be simple, but it's not complicated. This realization led me to develop the Legacy Leader Cultural Intelligence Accelerator

Model. It aims at providing a road map that can enable leaders to improve on their CQ and leverage it to build organizations that are also culturally intelligent.

More than two decades ago, Daniel Goleman highlighted the importance of emotional intelligence in leadership, telling the *Harvard Business Review*, "The most effective leaders are all alike in one crucial way: They all have a high degree of what has come to be known as emotional intelligence. It's not that IQ and technical skills are irrelevant. They do matter, but they are the entry-level requirements for executive positions." Over the past twenty-five years, the idea of EQ has become well ingrained in our corporate psyche. To be emotionally intelligent means having the ability of being sensitive to and perceptive of other people's emotions, while at the same time being able to intuitively facilitate improved performance based on this knowledge. Goldman insisted that possessing emotional intelligence is important because it allows leaders to better understand and motivate people.

Over the past nearly three decades, many training courses and countless coaching hours have been dedicated to helping leaders develop a high level of EQ. It is now part of the corporate vernacular. When we are asked to list the traits of great leaders, we often name emotional intelligence as one of the top criteria on the list. Recruiters use is as determinant factor in placing executive candidates, and companies use is as one of the important criteria for leadership competency and advancement to higher organizational levels. If you understand the importance and value of EQ, then the importance and value of CQ becomes readily evident.

Cultural intelligence has a link to EQ and IQ. However, it goes beyond emotional intelligence, and certainly is not a direct function of intellectual ability. We all know very intelligent people with poorly developed or awkward social skills. We probably have seen very emotionally intelligent people who can recognize, understand, and manage their emotions, and know how to positively (or negatively) influence the emotions of others, but who are unsure of themselves when they are in a foreign environment.

High-IQ and high-EQ people who have never been exposed to different cultures and diversity of people that often comes with working or living in various environments will likely have a low CQ level to begin with. That's to be expected. Fortunately, as we've already learned, it can be corrected and improved.

In chapter 2, we listed several of benefits of having a healthy level of CQ for a leader. Let's expand on a few of these ideas. A high-CQ leader will

o *gain respect quickly*. High-CQ leaders will gain respect from their teams across geographic and cultural boundaries more quickly if they are perceived to be culturally sensitive, aware, and adaptable. Respected leaders are more effective at moving their organizations to action.

o *quickly drive alignment of objectives*. Leaders with high CQ are able to gain alignment with their teams more readily than those perceived to have lower levels of cultural awareness. One of the most significant momentum killers in any team is the wasted energy spent trying to coalesce a group of people on objectives. Teams often waste more time arguing about how to do something, when in fact what they should be doing is aligning on where they are going. The "where" is the leader's end goal, not the "how." There is almost always more than one way to get the objectives accomplished; thus, the best leaders don't foster an environment where teams spend energy over-debating how to get it done. We have all heard of the expression "analysis paralysis." It happens often, and it's a momentum killer. Essentially, we are talking about the difference between driving agreement versus alignment. To put it bluntly, agreement is only a "nice to have". Alignment is a must. We don't need to agree on every decision, every single approach, or every action taken. However, we need to be aligned and equally motivated on what the end goal is.

Think of it this way: Imagine you are managing a project meeting. During the meeting, you are making important decisions on the work the team is doing to achieve the objectives. If it's a good meeting, there will be a healthy debate and even some arguing among the team members on what should be done next. There will also be a debate on how it should be done. At some point, a decision has to be made on how to proceed. That usually falls on the leader: you. You make the decision and adjourn the meeting so the work can go on. What if members of the team who did not agree on the approach that was chosen left the room and did not support the activities that were discussed? Maybe they did not do so purposefully, but in their action or inaction, they were not truly all-in working towards the objectives. Clearly, that would be less than ideal for any team. Realistically, this happens much of the time, and it's indicative of having a culture of trying to get to agreement rather than alignment. As a leader, what you need and expect is that when the decision is made, all members of the team align and work together to make it happen. However, this doesn't not happen on its own or by accident. It takes high-CQ leaders who are best equipped to get teams aligned on the goal.

o *create cultures of collaboration rather than negotiation.* Building on the previous point on the importance of aligning teams, we also need to understand the fundamental difference between collaboration and negotiation. The premise of negation is based on what can be described as an "I win, you lose," outcome-based methodology. Effective negotiation aims at settling differences between people. It's a process of achieving compromise while avoiding arguments or additional conflict. The goal by each party negotiating is to achieve what is best for them. Therein lies the problem with negotiation: It's about what is best for me and not necessarily what is best for us. One of the steps in negotiation is referred to as bargaining. For me, that conjures memories of going to a flea market and negotiating a price with a vendor for some item or other. You try to seem as disinterested in the item as you can, and they try hard not be too concerned about closing the sale with you. It's a game of chicken to see who will blink first and make the offer to name a price lower than the asking. You begin to walk away, and then you hear the vendor say, "Hang on, what about ..." and you smile within because you think you've won. Eventually, you agree on a price they are willing to accept, and you pay an amount you are willing to pay, even though it may be higher than what you had hoped for. That transaction, a result of your negotiations, sounds like a lose-lose outcome to me. Neither of you got exactly what you wanted. This is because your objectives were not aligned. Perhaps as you read this, you were reminded of a similar experience you may have lived. If you are like me, you may even enjoy these exchanges. For some of us, it's all part of the fun. However, when it comes to getting teams to achieve great things together, you don't want negotiation going on. You want collaboration.

The definition of *collaboration* is found in the spelling of the word: *col-labor-ation*. It means to colabor, to work together to produce something. Specifically, it's a working practice, whereby individuals work together to achieve a common goal, which will yield a mutually beneficial result. When we colabor, we focus on what we want to achieve and less on how we are going to do it. We apply principles such as trust, respect, and effective communications between us to align on the end goal, and we empower and support each other to achieve it. The difference between collaboration and negotiation is as clear as night and day. A high-CQ leader understands these differences and is effectively able to create a culture where collaboration rules and results are achieved for the benefit of the team.

There are also benefits to the broader organization when the leader models a high level of CQ. Listing just a few, high-CQ leaders will

o   create an organization of global thinkers,
o   foster a culture of respect and affection between colleagues and coworkers,
o   build teams (and people) with an ability to communicate despite language and cultural barriers that often slow progress in organizations, and
o   transform the company to become a talent magnet as it gains a reputation for being a culturally intelligent organization that leverages and values diversity and inclusion of talent across all differences.

Some aspects of CQ come naturally to most people. Most leaders who are at least somewhat intellectually curious will have an innate cultural intelligence level, and with work, they can attain a higher level of CQ. One thing is certain, leaders with low CQ will be at a distinct disadvantage in the global business world that is today the norm. Leaders therefore have great incentives to develop a high CQ level, model the appropriate behaviors, and enable a high-CQ culture across all levels of their organization.

Cultural intelligence is a must-have strength and trait of an effective leader. Today's global environment demands it. High-CQ leaders can effectively adapt to multicultural situations and use their understanding of the diversity within their team to build strategies that drive breakthrough results. The Legacy Leader CQ Accelerator Model (figure 1) provides an actionable road map to enable leaders to develop higher levels of CQ and then put it to work to create culturally intelligent organizations that will be more effective and achieve accelerated results. In subsequent chapters, we will detail each part of the model and suggest ways that each of us can accelerate our path to high CQ.

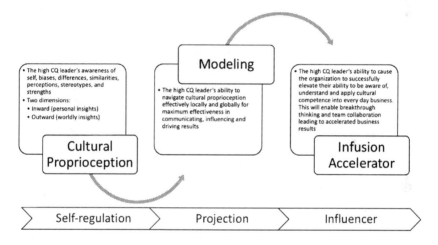

Figure 1: The Legacy Leader CQ Accelerator Model

CHAPTER 5

Cultural Proprioception

The Hollywood blockbuster movie *The Sixth Sense* made its debut in 1999. Now a classic, it's probably best known for one short line spoken by the youngest character in the movie. The line "I see dead people" was uttered by child actor Haley Joel Osment. All these years later, that's what most people quote of the American supernatural psychological thriller film written and directed by M. Night Shyamalan. The movie is about Malcom Crowe, a child psychologist whose patient, Cole Sear, can talk to the dead. Throughout the movie, Dr. Crowe works with Cole, trying to help him deal with his social skills, especially after seeing signs of physical harm. Cole finally confides his secret to Malcolm that he sees ghosts walking around like the living, unaware that they are dead. As the story unfolds, the many plot twists and surprising ending keep the audience at the edge of their seat. If you have not seen the movie, search it on Netflix, pop some kettle corn, and snuggle up on your couch to take in the thriller. Spoiler alert: Towards the end of the movie, Malcolm starts to see things he did not see earlier. He recalls being shot, locates his gunshot wound, and discovers he died that night from the wound and has been dead the entire time he was working with Cole. Malcolm tells his wife she was never second to anything and that he loves her. Malcolm's business is finally complete, and his spirit departs in a flash of light.

Now, it's movie trivia time: Why name the movie *The Sixth Sense*? Depending on what psychologist you ask, you may get a different answer to the question "What are the human senses?" The numbers range from five to twenty-one. Most, however, agree that we have six senses: sight, hearing, smell, taste, touch, and the lesser known proprioception.

The medical definition of proprioception is the ability to sense stimuli arising within the body regarding position, motion, and equilibrium. It's what gives even a blindfolded person the ability to know if her arm is above her head or hanging by the side of the body. Proprioception is from the Latin *proprius*, meaning "one's own, individual," and *capio, capere*, "to take or grasp." Thus, to grasp one's own position in space, including the position of the limbs in relation to each other and the body as a whole. Also referred to as kinaesthesia, proprioception encompasses three aspects known as the "ABC" of proprioception. These are agility, balance, and coordination. Without these, we would struggle to manage our day-to-day activities.

In the movie, Dr. Crowe clearly was lacking a sense of proprioception, and therefore his perception of reality was warped. Moreover, throughout the movie, he acted in accordance to what he perceived to be true that wasn't. He interacted with others based on those beliefs. His judgment was therefore flawed because his assumptions were wrong. Imagine if we behaved based on a set of assumptions that we believed to be true but were simply incorrect or incomplete. We too would be taking actions, albeit well-intentioned ones, that may be completely inappropriate for the situation we are dealing with. This is why I believe the journey to cultural intelligence for a leader has to begin with what I have defined as cultural proprioception.

As it relates to CQ, we define cultural proprioception as "the leader's awareness of self—and others—in terms of styles, biases, differences, stereotypes, strengths, and other behavioral norms that describe the environment they find themselves in."

The goal is for the leader to possess a high degree of cultural proprioception. Let's begin by understanding how we develop cultural proprioception. I believe it starts with becoming increasingly self-aware, because self-awareness leads to self-actualization, which leads to self-fulfillment and ultimately to happiness. You can't achieve that without being your authentic and unfiltered self. You can't become the high-CQ individual you are meant to be without having that crystal-clear picture of who you are, where you come from, and how you show up.

Becoming Increasingly Self-Aware

Self-awareness is having a clear perception of what our personality is like. It means understanding our strengths, weaknesses, triggers, and biases. Being self-aware means that we are in tune with our emotions, our attitudes, and how we are perceived by others. Over the course of my professional career, I have had the opportunity to be studied and analyzed with the help of a number of instruments, from Meyer-Briggs to Insights, to DISC, and many others. Moreover, I have taken these assessments at different periods and stages of my career. Throughout, I saw movement and improvements in many aspects of my personality and emotional intelligence skills. That is to be expected as we gain experiences and mature personally and professionally. What is also true is that some of our spots never change. These areas become things we learn to manage and in some cases even leverage, as we interact on a daily basis. What these instruments are also good at highlighting is how we behave when under stress. They teach us to be aware of our tendencies and behaviors, and even how our deep-rooted belief system rushes to the surface when we are in stressful situations. The best leaders are constantly on a journey of becoming increasingly self-aware, and they learn how to manage their behaviors to achieve their objectives.

Developing Cultural Proprioception

Most people have a fair idea of who they are and how they are perceived by others. We may not always like the answer from the person in the mirror, but if we ask ourselves some honest questions, it's likely that we have a rather clear perspective on our strengths and weaknesses. One thing is certain: Our view of the world and of ourselves, at least in the early stages of our lives, will be quite dependent on where and how we were raised. How much that view changes as we journey through life will depend on at least three things: what experiences we are exposed to, what we learn from those experiences, and our willingness to allow those lessons to alter our beliefs and actions going forward. That's the nature of cultural proprioception. It's starts with understanding our self very well, but it does not end there. We must journey beyond that understanding to explore how we show up based who we are and how we are perceived based on our behaviors.

If we are to develop higher levels of cultural proprioception, we must understand several enabling drivers:

- o understanding your own cultural identity and value systems
- o recognizing your own biases
- o accepting that you are susceptible to your biases
- o working to replace biases with tolerant thoughts and constructive behaviors
- o taking action to develop higher levels of cultural proprioception

Let's explore these further.

Understanding Cultural Identities and Value Systems

Cultural value systems are the core ideals upon which an entire community exists. It includes their traditional customs and rituals, their beliefs, and their guiding principles. It's what joins us as a part of a tribe; those shared characteristics often include religion, place of birth, and language. It goes beyond the obvious and extends to social behaviors and how they perceive art and literature. Of course, cultural identities stretch to cuisine and even the perception of aesthetics and how people look. It informs how they educate members of the tribe and the social ethics of expected and appropriate behaviors. It dictates how they organize the family unit, and it drives their business and legal practices. In other words, it's how they do things. Importantly, like it or not, it also dictates how this group is perceived by members of other tribes.

Understanding the tribe we come from is fundamental to understanding ourselves. We may not even be aware how much of this value system is manifested in our daily walk, but it is. Failure to recognize that fact will result in our inability to leverage the benefits of our value system, while managing the potential detractors of the same value system according to the situation and environment we find ourselves in at that moment. The smartest leaders, the high-CQ ones, grasp this idea at its core. They understand that the more they know who they are, how they show up, and how others may perceive them, the better they can be at managing their style situationally to the benefit of their objectives.

Recognizing Your Own Biases

Developing cultural proprioception can't happen if we don't recognize and deal with our biases. Biases anchor us down and distort our ability to be open-minded and consider new information that may inform us on what we believe and how we behave.

Consider the image in figure 2 below. How many triangles can you count?

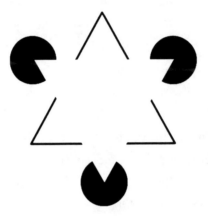

Figure 2. The Kanizsa Triangle

I have asked hundreds of people that same question. The most common answer I get is eight. But some have seen as many as twelve triangles. I then ask them this question: "Would you be willing to bet me a bottle of fine cabernet wine? Are you that sure of your response?" Invariably, some agree on the bet. Invariably, they lose. The correct answer is zero. There are no triangles in figure 2. A triangle is a polygon with three connected edges and three vertices. Not all three edges of what appear as triangles to some of us are actually connected. The Kanizsa triangle is an optical illusion first described by the Italian psychologist Gaetano Kanizsa in 1955. It is also known as a subjective or illusory contour illusion. The study of the Kanizsa triangle, along with other visual and perceptual illusions, has led to greater understanding of how the brain and eyes perceive visual information. Thus, what most see as triangles is, instead, three oddly placed Vs and three Pacmen. Moreover, some are so sure they see triangles that they are willing to take an action, in this case, place a bet, based on that belief. Since their assumption was wrong, their action was incorrect, and they suffered the consequence. That simple exercise is the best way that I have found to explain the concept of unconscious bias.

Unconscious biases are social stereotypes about groups of people that we form outside our conscious awareness. They are learned stereotypes that are automatic, unintentional, deeply engrained, and able to influence our behavior. Unconscious biases are activated involuntarily and often without our awareness or intentional control because they reside deep in the subconscious. Perhaps the worst thing about unconscious biases is that left unchecked, they can cause poor decisions in our personal and professional lives.

Accepting That You Are Susceptible to Your Biases

The word *bias* often conjures negative images and thoughts. It's not hard to understand why that's the case, given our politically and racially charged global environment. However, bias is neither good nor bad. In fact, they can come with upsides. A bias is a disproportionate weight in favor of or against an idea, a person, a group, or a thing, usually in a way that is closed-minded, prejudicial, or unfair. Biases are learned. People may develop biases for or against an individual, a group, or a belief. Biases, often informed by a stereotype, can lead to prejudicial behaviors. Given that a prejudice is an opinion against a group or individual based on insufficient facts, it's no surprise it often yields negative results.

There are many forms of biases, and as many definitions of what they are. One of the simplest ways to described them is three types:

o *Like Me bias*: That is a preference for those more like us.
o *Confirmation bias*: This refers to how people primarily search for bits of evidence that back up their opinions, rather than

looking at the whole picture. People often subconsciously slip into confirmation bias because they seek confirmation that their initial assessment of a person is correct.

o *Anchor bias*: This is based on the first thing we learn about something or someone sets the bias. Most often, it comes from our childhood experiences and what we were taught to believe about a group or a person.

One other way that biases are defined is as either explicit or implicit. Explicit bias, also known as conscious bias, is where people are very clear about their feelings about someone else and behave accordingly with intent. Implicit bias is another way of referring to unconscious bias, which we already discussed. Whether conscious or unconscious, biases are pervasive. Everyone possesses them, even people with avowed commitments to impartiality, such as judges. Interestingly, we generally tend to hold implicit biases that favor our own ingroup, though research has shown that we can hold implicit biases against our ingroup. It's also noteworthy that implicit biases are malleable, meaning the implicit associations we have formed in our brain can be gradually unlearned.

It's not my intent to oversimplify or minimize the complexity and the impact of biases, prejudices, and intolerance that exist. These biases lead to many of the problems our society has experienced in the past and continues to deal with today. I am by no means an expert on the subject and do not pretend that these few paragraphs on bias and its impact on society at large are a sufficient academic treatment of this topic. However, I do forcefully contend the following points as it relates to leadership and how leaders deal with their bias: First, we must accept that we have biases and that they can influence our behaviors. Second, we must do everything we can to overcome our biases if we expect to become the most effective leaders we can be.

Work to Replace Biases with Tolerant Thoughts and Constructive Behaviors

Some months ago, I had an experience that at first brought a smile to my face, only to be followed by a frown as I realized what it meant. It was the middle of the night, and I got out of bed to head to the bathroom. Fortunately, it's not something that happens often. I remember slipping my feet into slippers that were at the foot of my bed. Without turning on the lights, I began to make my way across the hardwood floor to the bathroom. As I shuffled my feet, barely lifting them off the floor as I walked, the slippers made a sound that can only be described as a "shush shush shush." About halfway to the bathroom, I stopped, and immediately my mind traveled nearly fifty years into the past. I recalled hearing my grandmother's feet shuffling across the floor in the middle of the night as she made her way to the one bathroom in her small house in Yauco, Puerto Rico. I smiled for a quick moment. Then I frowned as I thought to myself, *Oh, my goodness, I've turned into my grandmother.*

Have you had a similar moment? That point when you realize that in some ways, not always good, you are more like your mom or your dad, or someone else who influenced you, than you care to admit?

If you want to know where your bias come from, you need only look back on your childhood. Who said what? What did they do? How did people around you behave towards others? What did your teacher say in class? What did your priest or pastor teach from the pulpit? What was going on in the world? What was on the news? What movies where popular? How about music? How do you feel about people of other races? What about your feelings on people from certain religions, political affiliations, ideologies, or sexual preferences? These are tough and uncomfortable questions that we must deal with. Chances are, all of these sorts of influences shaped who you are today, how you think, and in many ways how you behave. Good or bad, these things are hardwired into our brains. Managing our beliefs requires being in touch with them so that, when necessary, we can modify them and learn new ways of thinking and behaving.

Here are a few techniques you can practice to overcome your biases:

- recognize and accept that you have bias
- get out of your comfort zone
- explore awkwardness and discomfort
- engage with people you consider "others"
- increase your contact with the different groups
- avoid stereotypes and over-generalizations
- separate feelings from facts
- have diverse people around the decision-making table
- engage in self-reflection to uncover personal biases
- humbly seek feedback from people in other groups

There is one more technique that we can practice that will help us manage our bias. In my experience, it is the most powerful of them all and can be stated in two words: suspend judgment.

According to research, in just 600 milliseconds, the human brain can think of a word, apply the rules of grammar to it, and send it to the mouth to be spoken. Moreover, the physiological reason our minds wander, even when we try to listen, is because the human brain is capable of processing words at a much higher speed than a person is able to speak. The average rate of speech for an American is about 125 words per minute, while the human brain can process about 800 words per minute. So we have two problems: The first one is that the time it takes for a thought to get to our mouth is a fraction of a second. The second problem is that our brain is processing words faster than we can speak them. Put those two things together, and what we have is a perfect recipe for saying the wrong thing fast. If only we would pause for a moment. This would allow our brain to consider all the information that is being presented, run it through a filter to remove our own bias that may be corrupting the thought, and formulate a well-articulated sentence or two that our mouth can then elegantly express. This can all happen, if we simply suspend judgment for a moment to ensure that we are not responding to whatever it is we are hearing or experiencing at that moment with anything other than objectivity and fact-based reasoning. Stop and think; it only takes a second.

Taking Action to Develop Higher Levels of Cultural Proprioception

Now that we've dealt with the things that can block us from developing a high level of cultural proprioception, let talk specifically about what we can do to develop it further. There are two areas we should explore: inward and outward proprioception. As the words imply, one has to do with what is and comes from within us. Essentially, it's what we do to continue to get connected with who we are, how we show up, and how we can be perceived. It's us dealing with our biases and managing our behaviors. Outward proprioception refers to us furthering our understanding of the world around us. It's our global or worldly insights gained from what we learn via education and personal experiences.

Inward Proprioception

To develop inward proprioception, first and foremost we need to tackle the implicit and explicit biases we previously discussed. That action, more than any other, will enable our CQ excellence journey. Keep in mind, these are the beliefs that anchor us, most times not in a good way. Here are a few other ways we can go about developing our inward proprioception:

o *Remain intellectually curious.* An intellectually curious person has the willingness and desire to learn new things and dig deeper than what is seen on the surface. This curiosity is innate in some of us and not so natural in others. If you find yourself often asking the question why, that's a good sign you have a healthy level of curiosity. If you go beyond that and ask probing questions, looking to peel back layers of information as you seek to understand, chances are you're an intellectually curious person. Intellectually curious people take things apart just because they want to know how they work. They enjoy figuring things out and demonstrate a genuine interest in simply expanding their understanding of the world around them.

At the risk of stating the obvious, intellectual curiosity is important. With the few exceptions of accidental innovations, inventions, and discoveries, all major accomplishments, technological or otherwise, have an intellectually curious individual behind them. Being an intellectually curious person keeps your mind thinking actively and makes you more observant to new ideas. It allows you to see new possibilities and frankly makes you more interesting. Think about those last two sentences carefully. The key words in those sentences are "thinking actively," "more observant," "see new possibilities," and "more interesting." I don't know about you, but I see these as great qualities in a leader.

Thus, given its importance, how do you develop intellectual curiosity? There are many ways. Here are a few ways to develop intellectual curiosity: first, learn to listen well and ask questions relentlessly. Second, if you think something is boring, challenge yourself to figure out how to make it less mundane. Third, keep an open mind and avoid distractions (read multitasking) when listening. Fourth, and most importantly, learn to ask why effectively. This is the leader's secret weapon.

o *Learn to ask why?* When you ask the question why, depending on how you ask it, there can be unintended consequences. Leaders need to be especially sensitive to this fact. If a leader asks, "Why did you do that?", it may indicate to the person being asked that the leader is not happy with the outcome that caused them to ask the question. "Why" can be a provocative word and may put some people on the defensive. Asking why with an aggressive tone is certainly not going to solicit the same response as asking it in a more friendly way. So how can we you ask why without creating that impression? Simple. Change the words. Saying something like, "That's interesting, tell me more," gets a much warmer response to a poorly asked why. Another way to say it might be, "Help me understand why that works," or "I'm curious why that is. Go on." Asking why the right way can have a very motivational effect on the person being asked the question. They feel that you are listening to them and are interested in what they have to say.

o *Park your assumptions and stereotypes.* Rather than letting your preconceived notions about other cultures, traditions, and beliefs guide what you think and say at any moment, use every possible opportunity to test your knowledge before speaking. Listen first, then respond. Ask a question to buy your mind some time to form an intelligent thought before weighing in on a discussion. This action alone will set you apart from most people in the room.

o *Get out of your comfort zone.*

o *Slow down, suspend judgment, and abandon your biases.*

Outward Proprioception

Have you ever described anyone, perhaps even yourself, as worldly? What do we mean when we say that? People who are considered worldly are experienced about the social, political, economic, and practical aspects of life, beyond the small region of the world they come from. We all begin our life from somewhere in the world. For many, their entire life is spent near their birthplace. Others move around and live or work in different parts of the world. I have come to the realization that there are pros and cons to both of these lifestyles.

I grew up in Villa Carolina, Puerto Rico; Calle 50, Bloque 55, #11, Villa Carolina, Puerto Rico, 00630. That was my address from age three months until I was nearly sixteen years old. Over the many years since leaving there, I have returned on occasions to visit the old neighborhood. It's amazing to me how little it's changed. Within those few blocks where I roamed all of my formative years, there are still people I grew up with living in the same houses they did as children. Some left temporarily for career purposes and came back. A few others just never left and have lived their entire life in the same house. Some of us left and only come back for a visit from time to time. It was comforting to me to know that no matter when I would return, I would surely find Doña Panchita and Don Felix sitting in *la marquesina*, rocking in their chairs. Around the block, I would surely find Laura, one of my mom's friends, living in the same corner house. Sammy, Barry, and Tata, three of the kids I grew up with, would soon come around when word spread that *el perdido* (the lost one) had come to visit. We'd all gather around and catch up. They would be curious about where I had been and what part of the world I was living in now. They seemed fascinated by that.

I was anxious to hear about their life and found myself envying the deep roots and lifelong friendships they enjoyed. Pros and cons. Not one life better than the other, just different. I did, however, realize, in some cases, their thinking about issues or how they saw the world seemed a bit narrow-minded to me. No doubt their biases influenced the way they interpreted things, just like mine do. However, I believe that perhaps my perspective was more inclusive and even a bit less judgmental than theirs. Maybe I viewed the world from a different lens than they did because I had the opportunity to experience the world in a more direct way, having traveled to so many different regions of the globe. Could it be that I was just fortunate to have had the career opportunities that moved me around and exposed me to different people and ways of thinking? These experiences influenced my way of seeing the world and interacting. I concluded, the answer to that question is yes. However, it also led me to consider this question: How can someone develop that global mindset if they are not as fortunate to travel or be exposed to diversity of people, places, cultures, and social practices?

Developing our outward proprioception can be accelerated if we spend the time studying and learning about other cultures and people who are different from ourselves. Here are a few areas we can gain a working knowledge of these:

- o *Business and legal systems in different industrial sectors and regions of the world.* This would provide an understanding of how work is conducted and the economic considerations for that area.
- o *Traditional and cultural systems.* This would include religious, political, and educational processes and systems. Understanding them would broaden our views, lead us to consider the pros and cons of our own processes and systems, and perhaps help us to evolve our own ways of doing things.
- o *Social traditions.* Certainly, understanding things such as social etiquette, special holidays celebrated, the preferred music listened to for a group of people, a region of the country, or the world would enable us to fluidly interact and assimilate ourselves into their environment. Moreover, it can be a ton of fun to enjoy these differences.
- o *Language.* This is about how people express themselves, their mannerisms and the symbology they communicate with. A nod

of the head with certain cultures has a very specific meaning. A handshake versus a bow can mean the difference between a good meeting or a not-so-effective one in Japan. Importantly, the different meanings of the same word from one part of the world to another is easily the difference between a good conversation or an embarrassing moment. This is especially true with languages such as Spanish that is spoken in so many different parts of the USA and other countries as the primary language. Some words I use as part of the Spanish spoken in Puerto Rico can be very different in meaning to the same word spoken in Colombia or Mexico. I have experienced many funny moments with colleagues and friends from other parts of Latin America when we discovered the different meaning of the same word, depending on who said it.

o *Exercise intellectual curiosity.* We have spoken at length about the importance of being intellectually curious. We can demonstrate intellectual curiosity by being well read and informed about local, national, and international news. We can become familiar with cultural mannerisms and common colloquial phrases used by different people and, when possible, engage with people from different cultures who can educate us.

o *Immersion.* One of the easiest ways to increase your outward proprioception is to seek the opportunity for extensive global travel. If you have the opportunity to live in different cities, states, or countries, even for a short period of time, take advantage of it to learn as much as you can about that place and its people.

o *Participate in multicultural events, and attend different church services.*

o *Remain open-minded.* Learn and practice the idea of suspending judgment and thinking before acting.

o *Work to detach (not abandon) from your own culture.* Getting outside of ourselves and becoming comfortable with being out of our comfort zone will start to feel increasingly stimulating and enjoyable. This is something we can do without losing our authenticity. It's not about abandoning who we are, where we come from, or the way we do things in order to assimilate to someone else's way of doing things. It is about integrating the two ideals where possible to create a stronger and more effective communication channel between the two parties.

True to Self: Remaining Authentic

The Prosperity Table

A few years into my tenure at Ansell Healthcare, I found myself in the beautiful city of Seoul, South Korea. We were inaugurating a new office there, and the entire Ansell team was very excited to participate in the grand opening. I was too. It wasn't so much that the office was very large or opulent. In fact, it was quite a modest space. However, it was an indication of growth and investment by the company and the small team of dedicated employees in Korea, which was worth celebrating. When we arrived at the office for the dedication, I was impressed with how well they had prepared for the occasion. I was expecting the typical "say a few words" and ribbon cutting, but this was much more than that. The team had organized a traditional Korean celebration and blessing ceremony to commemorate the occasion. Part of this tradition included preparing what was described as the prosperity table. The table had food and fruit, as well as some other items. Most notably, there was a large pig head at the center of the table.

The ceremony was kicked off by the host. He was going to walk the team through the rituals that involved reading some prayers the team leader was to repeat. It also involved having that same leader kneel before the table, recite some additional prayers while at times bowing before the table as a sign of respect. I was standing close to the moderator, where I had been instructed to wait for my cue to indicate it was my turn to participate in the ritual. As the leader of the organization, it was important for the team to see me involved. Prior to starting the event, I was briefed on what I was expected to do. I asked a few questions to understand the meaning of each of the rituals and ensure that I would be comfortable with their significance. I was not trying to judge their beliefs or alter them in any way. I was, however, making sure they did not conflict with my Christian beliefs or violate any of my fundamental tenets. The host was happy to explain all they were going to do and gladly answered the few questions I asked. There was only one part of the ritual I felt a bit uncomfortable with. Before I asked to be excused from participating for that portion, he was very quick to suggest that my Korean colleague do that part on my behalf. We proceeded, and when the ceremony was completed, we enjoyed a very festive day with the team, which culminated in a fantastic dinner later that evening.

It wasn't until after dinner, while we were saying our goodbyes prior to my departure, that I realized the impact of my participation in the day's ceremony. One of the younger members of the Korean team wanted a selfie picture with me, and I happily obliged. Soon one picture turned into two, then three, and before long, we were all crowded together taking pictures. The same young man then said loudly, "It was really good to see you participate in our ceremony today. Maybe you're part Korean?" We all laughed. "Yes, it was great that you were a part of it," said another team member. "Thank you. It's good to see our leaders involved that way."

Her English may have not been perfect, but her message hit the mark with me. It would have been easy and perfectly acceptable to them, had I opted to be a bystander during the ceremony. Perhaps that is what they expected. However, modeling the willingness to be all-in is noticed by all. If leaders are willing to do it, they surely will be open to seeing the world through other lenses as well. Importantly, as leaders, we can do this without violating our authenticity or doing anything in direct conflict with our personal beliefs.

The leader's journey to high cultural intelligence begins with developing a high degree of cultural proprioception and learning to self-regulate behaviors. Leaders who do this well will move to the subsequent two steps in process, effectively lead their organizations, and enable them to build the foundation of a high-CQ team.

CHAPTER 6

Modeling

Resplendent Island, Teardrop of India, and Pearl of the Indian Ocean. These are a few of the nicknames of the beautiful country of Sri Lanka. While I was president of Ansell Healthcare, I had the pleasure of visiting this beautiful place on many occasions. I created such wonderful memories thanks to the incredibly warm, hard-working people of the Ansell manufacturing plant. From the very first time I visited the plant, and how I was received, it was a true learning experience for me. I grew immensely with each of the interactions I had with members of the team in this great company.

I recall the moment the company car went through the gate of the plant, and the guards standing at attention saluting the vehicle as it passed, something they did for dignitaries when they visited the plant. In my mind, I was immediately transported to when I was a US Air Force officer and was entering a gated area of a base. The guards would wave us in with a hand-salute. I thought, *Wow, that's cool.* A few seconds later, the car pulled up in front of the plant's lobby. The entire leadership staff was standing there, waiting to greet the new boss. There were a few women in traditional dresses, waiting to welcome me and David Lucas, the vice president of R&D, who was traveling along with me. As I stepped out of the car and approached them, not quite sure what do to, they smiled and said, "Welcome." They handed me some neatly stacked green leaves.

I reached for them, held them in my palm, smiled, and said, "Thank you." A second later, I smiled again at her and asked, "Is there something special I should do with these?"

She smiled. "No," she said, "it's just our way of saying hello."

I held on to the leaves in my left hand and proceeded to shake hands with everyone I was meeting for the first time with my right hand. We made our way upstairs into the conference room, and waiting there was fresh cold coconut with a straw already in it.

"We heard you like coconut water, so we thought we'd have one waiting for you."

I was immediately in love with these folks. I could only hope I was making as good a first impression on them as they were on me.

Over the next few years, I would experience many incredible things while in Sri Lanka. I had fun experiencing the local culture, tasting Sri Lankan cuisine, and trying to pick up just a bit of the Sinhala language. Visiting an elephant sanctuary and seeing some of the more remote parts of the island left a special imprint on me. Special to me were the long walks we took as we inspected the different parts of the plant and visited the employees at their workstations. I also listened to employees boast about the progress they were making in their manufacturing processes as they stood in front of an easel with posters updating me on some project or other. Their enthusiasm was contagious. They spoke English, although it was obvious that some of them struggled with the language. That didn't stop them. I listened carefully, sometimes asking them to slow down or repeat something. They would gently apologize for their English not being "so good."

I would smile and say, "Your English is just fine. I just can't think that fast."

They would laugh and go on with their presentation.

Planting a coconut tree in the Sri Lanka manufacturing site was a significant highlight for me. Many trees have been planted on site by visiting leaders and other important guests. Each time I visited, we had the ceremonial watering of the tree, and I saw how big it was getting with each passing visit. I miss that and hope one day I have the opportunity to return to see it and maybe even taste a coconut from that tree. Of all the wonderful experiences, three stand out as most impactful for me. As I have pondered on these memories many times over, I am gratified to think that perhaps, in some small way, I made a difference to the people there. Perhaps as they observed their leader behaving in a certain way, they too would see things through a different filter and alter some of their beliefs and behaviors. Not because my way was better than theirs or theirs better than mine, but because we learned from one another, adjusted, and accommodated to one another. In doing so, we created a better relationship.

One Small Change

I visited the Sri Lanka plant every couple of months. After the first few times, the team and I had gotten to know each other quite well and developed a bit of a routine. One afternoon, we were having a meeting in the conference room regarding several human resource topics. At the time, the staff was composed of mostly men. The only woman on the senior leadership team was the director of human resources. During the meeting, the discussion turned to the issues being confronted in one manufacturing team specifically. It seemed they were having some performance and retention challenges. Everyone kept referring to the "girls" in the department. "The girls are saying …", or "The girls are trying to …". It wasn't meant with any disrespect at all, none that I could perceive, anyway. The only woman in the room used the same terminology. As I listened carefully, I learned that department was historically composed strictly of women. No men had ever worked in the department or even applied to work in that department.

After a bit of debate and discussion of suggested solutions to the problem, the group decided it was time for a tea break. During the break, I asked Hasith, the plant general manager, if we could have a quick chat. I had gotten to know him over the past six months and really liked him. I found him to be a good, hard-charging leader with great potential to grow personally and professionally. I also thought he could do a good job for the plant, as it had many challenges ahead. During our quick chat, I asked him to do me a favor. Of course, he agreed immediately, not even waiting to know what I was about to ask.

I said, "I'd like you to try to change one thing in how you refer to members of the team. Rather than refer to them as girls, I'd like to ask you to use the word 'women' instead."

At first, he looked at me a bit perplexed. I think he was trying to figure out if I was just kidding. I imagine he might have been thinking, *What's the difference?*

I went on to explain, "I just think that we should try to be more respectful of them and refer to them as women rather than girls. In my way of thinking, we usually refer to girls when they are kids or very young, not when they are professionals working at the company."

I am not sure if he agreed or whether he believed it would make a difference, but he agreed to do it.

I went on to say, "Let's ask the rest of the team to do the same, okay?"

When we returned to the meeting, the next time he referred to members of the team, Hasith used the word "women" instead of "girls." That was my cue. I interrupted briefly, and being careful not to create an awkward moment, I went on to thank Hasith for using this new terminology when referring to women working in the plant. I said a few more words about how I thought this would show a bit more respect towards them and asked each of the leaders in the room to model that behavior.

After a quick moment of silence and a few nods of agreement from the men in the room, there was a collective "Sure," and the meeting went on. I made brief eye contact with the only woman in the room, and she had a Mona Lisa smile on her face. Subtle, but I could tell she was pleased. Throughout the meeting, someone would slip and say "girls" instead of "women," and the group would catch him and call him out, all in good humor. I thought this could be the beginning of a broader change. All these years later, I don't know if that stuck and made a permanent change in the plant. I hope it at least changed a few minds.

Modeling Impacts Behaviors

Modeling behavior leads to imitation and learning. The attitude, tone, style, and indeed the very personality of a leader are under constant observation and evaluation by everyone in the organization. Highly ethical leaders expect and only accept ethical behavior by their team members. Leaders who behave with a high degree of emotional intelligence, demonstrating a level-headed approach even under crisis conditions, can expect their team will likely respond with a certain level of control, even under stress. Leaders who are seen as participating in and enjoying cultural rituals or traditions during company events or while attending a business meeting in a foreign country, will see that people in the organization will be more open to doing the same. The contrary of these last three statements is also true. It's really that simple. People imitate leaders. Therefore, the most effective leaders work diligently at modeling the right behaviors consistently, living the stated values of the organization, and acting in ways that promote an inclusive culture that leverages the strengths of all members of the team.

Leaders who possess a high level of cultural intelligence are able to quickly connect to their organizations and more effectively gain alignment to the vision and mission. They also play an important role in educating their colleagues, peers, and the teams below them by modeling the behaviors that support a high-CQ organizational culture. They enable cultures where diversity is not just nice to have but a business imperative. They leverage diversity as a competitive advantage and drive inclusion as the operational modus operandi.

As the Legacy Leader Cultural Acceleration Model implies, in this stage, we expect the leader to project the right behaviors to enable others in the organization to improve on their individual cultural proprioception. The cumulative impact of each person's CQ adds to a higher CQ level for the entire organization.

Projecting the Right Stuff

We define *modeling* as the high-CQ leader's ability to navigate cultural proprioception effectively locally and globally for maximum effectiveness in communicating, influencing, and driving results. The idea is relatively simple and reminiscent of the Situational Leadership Model (SLM). In the

SLM, leaders decide which style of leadership to apply, choosing among supporting, coaching, delegating, and directing styles. Importantly, before choosing which style to use in a given situation, leaders must also consider the follower's readiness (e.g., are they able to do it or not) and their willingness (e.g., are they willing to do it or not). Similarly, as it relates to modeling the right behaviors, leaders need to be sensitive to the cultural factors in the environment they are in at the moment.

A leader would wisely choose a different approach, and even tone of voice, when communicating to employees in Tokyo versus delivering the same message (in terms of communication points) to an audience in Malaysia. The cultural difference, and the way in which these audiences would hear the message, are clearly different. Thus, modeling a high level of CQ includes being able to see through the lenses and hear through the filters of the people the leader is trying to influence.

Additionally, to model high-CQ behaviors, leaders need to demonstrate a healthy dose of the following traits:

o   Empathy: Leaders need to demonstrate they can be comfortable in different cultural settings and that they are able to see the world through another person's perspective.

o   Adaptability: Leaders need to be able to change their style, tone, demeanor, and body language to appropriately match the environment.

o   Flexibility: Leaders must demonstrate the ability to change course and tolerate ambiguity and uncertainty.

o   Friendliness: This is how approachable leaders are perceived to be. People will judge their overall demeanor and determine whether they seem to be genuinely enjoying interactions in different cultural environments.

o Sensitivity: Leaders must be able to demonstrate that they understand other's feelings and are in tune with the subtleties involved in multicultural interactions.

Modeling an Evolving Mindset

There is one other important idea for leaders to consider as it relates to developing and then modeling cultural intelligence. Leaders must model a behavior of consistent learning and evolving as individuals, being open-minded and curious about others and their way of thinking. Behaving and demonstrating a willingness to adapt and change our own behaviors as we grow personally is an important way that leaders can model an evolving mindset.

CQ can be cultivated and developed more easily than other personality traits. Leaders with a healthy level of IQ and EQ can constantly evolve their CQ level. Taking proactive steps to work to examine their CQ (as described earlier with the use of one or more instruments), leaders can establish a starting point for development. As with any developmental instrument, identifying a few areas to focus on first is the next step. Trying to alter too many behaviors at once will likely only lead to failure or frustration. Next, leaders should actively look for opportunity to place themselves in culturally diverse situations, forcing themselves to practice the learned skills and develop the muscle memory that will enable them to move fluidly from one environment to another. Finally, the smartest leaders surround themselves with people who will challenge them and provide them honest, direct, and timely feedback on how they are coping with the different situations and environments. They will also provide them feedback on how their interactions are being perceived and received. The bottom line is this: Developing a healthy and high level of CQ is within the reach of most people. Whether cultivated or innate, a leader with a demonstrated high CQ level will be a stronger and more effective leader, saying and doing the right things at the right time.

Modeling Values

Modeling the right behaviors starts with having a crystal-clear definition of values, both personal and organizational. Leaders must be clear on what their personal values are and be able to express them both in words and actions. It must be obvious to the organization why leaders hold these values dear and why they consider them important. This requires leaders to be authentic, honest, and consistent in everything they say and do.

Next, leaders need to link personal and organizational values: If they are different, these differences have to be reconciled and explained. Once there is alignment with the personal and organizational values, leaders can make intelligent choices on the behaviors they must exhibit to live those values. The actions leaders take in this regard must be specific and purposeful. A list of actions to start, stop, and continue can be helpful to keep leaders focused. Of course, leaders then hold themselves and others around them to the highest level of accountability against these values and expectations.

Finally, leaders should take a look in the mirror and ask themselves: How did I demonstrate our values today? Did I recognize or call out anyone who should have been for living our values? Am I being consistent day after day? Asking some simple questions and holding ourselves, and others, accountable to walking the values each day is a powerful way to ensure that we are modeling the right behaviors that ultimately create the organizational culture we are striving for.

The White Cotton Thread

This chapter began with a story about the wonderful Ansell team I was privileged to lead in Sri Lanka. My experiences there, and in so many other places I was fortunate to travel for work over the years, taught me valuable lessons that have shaped who I am today. I will end the chapter with another story from my time in Sri Lanka. I am reminded of the time we were inaugurating new manufacturing lines in our plant. These lines represented a significant capital investment by the company and were part of a long-term plan to transform the organization from the ground up. Many of the executives in my team traveled along with me to celebrate the occasion. As customary for special events such as these in Sri Lanka, the local Buddhist monk was invited to attend and offer a blessing over the people and facility.

For myself, and many of my colleagues, it was the first time we had experienced the rituals the monk was conducting as part of the celebration. Fortunately for us, we had great hosts who walked us through each step and narrated for us what was going on and what the meaning of it was. I noticed several of my teammates asking many questions. I too was curious and was asking my local colleague questions. I could tell from the expression on my teammates' faces that they were genuinely enjoying the moment. It was also obvious that our local hosts, many of whom are practicing Buddhist, were happy to be sharing their practices and customs with their visitors.

During one special moment in the celebration, after the monk had offered some customary prayers, and as the other monks in attendance continued to chant, people in the audience could go before the monk to receive a blessing. One by one, many of the local team members lined up to receive the blessing and have the monk tie a simple white cotton thread around their wrist. During my many visits to the plant, I often noticed people with a white thread tied around their wrist. I never thought much about it; I assumed it had some meaning but had never asked. This time, of course, I did ask.

Leaning into the plant manager, I whispered, "What does it mean to have a white string tied around the wrist?"

He smiled and said, "We believe it holds Buddha's blessing as long as it is tied around the wrist."

I nodded my understanding.

After a few minutes, the plant manager asked me, "Do you want to receive one?"

I thought about it and quickly responded, "Is that okay?"

He answered, "Of course, please do."

In my mind, having been raised a Roman Catholic, this process reminded me of the Communion Catholics partake as part of the Mass. As I thought about it, I imagined there was some prerequisite to being able to participate in receiving the blessing and having the string tied around the wrist. I thought perhaps you had to be a Buddhist or have somehow completed some training or other formal process. I was ascribing a Catholic mindset to the process. In the Roman Catholic religion, you are not really supposed to take Communion until after you have completed the sacrament of First Communion.

Intrigued and moved by what I was witnessing, I asked him again, "Are you sure it's okay?"

He said, "Yes, of course it is."

With that assurance, I made my way up to the line and followed what others were doing. Soon, a few other members of the visiting team were doing the same.

When I got back to my prior standing position, my host said, "Glad you did it. You should not remove the string. It will eventually break and fall off on its own."

The ceremony concluded, and we went on with the rest of our business day. We had learned something new, and I was pleased that many of the leaders I was traveling with had immersed themselves in the process. I know it created great memories for the local production workers who witnessed all of us fully participating.

The modeling stage of the CQ Accelerator Model may be the hardest one of the three. Leaders require a great deal of mental energy and focus to ensure they consistently set the right tone that will create the culture they are aiming for. This is why leaders must be constantly learning and curious; always seeking to understand the environment they are in, broadening their field of view, and proactively striving to learn lessons from all that is happening around them.

CHAPTER 7

Infusion Accelerator

The word *infusion* has an elegance to it. I especially like the medical interpretation of the word. In medicine, infusion deals with introducing fluids into the body via intravenous or subcutaneous application. Sometimes, an infusion pump is used to facilitate the process of getting fluids or medications into the bloodstream to treat all sorts of illnesses or help a patient combat dehydration or other ailments. The right infusion at the right time can literally be a lifesaver for the patient. An infusion delivers just the right amount of medication as indicated by the patient's condition. Drip, drip, drip. Sometimes a fast drip, sometimes a slower drip. As soon as it enters the body, the infused fluid becomes integrated with our blood. In the end, the medicine, antibiotics, or hydrating fluids, now mixed with our blood, hitch a ride through our circulatory system to deliver the medication to every part of the body in need of it. Most people who have ever received an infusion via an intravenous catheter will attest that the infusion itself, which is the fluid entering the body, does not hurt. However, getting the needle in the vein, well, that can be a bit painful.

I bet you know where I am going with this infusion analogy. It's a leader's job to infuse the right stuff into an organization. As in the case of a medication infusion, the patient's (read organization's) condition will determine the type of medicine (actions) that needs to be injected (modeled), the speed at which it is infused, and even over what period of time it will be required. Oh yes, one more thing just to take this infusion analogy to the edge of the comical: Leaders need to understand there might be some pain during the initial injection as they work to get the medicine to reach every part of the patient as quickly as possible. That is what being an infusion accelerator means to a high-CQ leader.

Leaders who have finely tuned cultural proprioception and consistently model the behaviors that promote cultural intelligence will become infusion accelerators and speed up their ability to influence the organization to achieve results. We define *infusion accelerator* as "the high-CQ leader's ability to cause the organization to successfully elevate their ability to be aware of, understand, and apply culture competence into everyday business practice." By their behavior, high-CQ leaders enable individuals in their organization to raise their own level of CQ, enjoy the benefits of a team that can collaborate more quickly across cultural and other differences, and achieve breakthroughs with speed that leads to results.

One, Two, Three, Infuse

There are three steps necessary for a leader to become an effective infusion accelerator, as illustrated in figure 3. Let's describe each of these steps in detail.

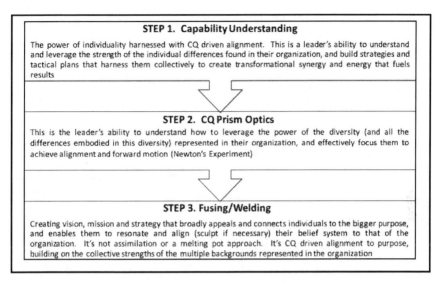

Figure 3: Three steps to becoming an infusion accelerator

Step 1: Capability Understanding: The Power of Individuality Harnessed with CQ-Driven Alignment

We define this capability understanding as "the leader's ability to understand and leverage the strength of the individual differences found in their organization and build strategies and tactical plans that harness these differences collectively to create transformational synergy and energy that fuel results."

At first, you may be tempted to think this first step would be especially important only in organizations that cross geographical borders with members of the team (or customers and business partners) who are located in different regions of the world. That is not the case. The reality is that even in what may seem as a relatively homogenous corporate environment, the diversity of the team is likely significant. Moreover, as the world has become smaller, many businesses have become increasingly global in the reach they can achieve with their products and services. Thus, capability understanding is important regardless of size, complexity, industry, sector, or type of business the organization is in. It's about people and getting them quickly aligned.

As leaders work with their senior teams to develop the strategies that will be communicated and implemented across the organization, they need to be sensitive to how these will resonate and be received in different cultural contexts. A simple example of this might be what happens when creating a company motto. If the motto (words, phrases, symbols) used are developed by a team that only speaks English, and they don't test the motto once translated into other languages, they may find the meaning is entirely different and perhaps not appropriate. Or they may find the value the motto expresses is either lost or misinterpreted in another language. This could send conflicting messages as to what is important to a company at its core.

From 2001 to 2006, the US Army launched a campaign using "An Army of One" as a tagline. The intent was likely to build the Army one soldier at a time. They probably wanted to indicate that each soldier was strong, well trained, and fully capable. The problem with that tagline is that the Army needs teams of soldiers and not lone rangers. The tagline was sending a confusing message and was not in synch with the true values of the US Army. Today, their website quotes "Serve with Honor. Live with Purpose." This is a much stronger call to action and consistent with the values that have defined the US Army for hundreds of years. This example illustrates the basic idea of aligning organizational values and messages to ensure they will be consistently interpreted in the way intended by the diverse audiences targeted by the message.

Effective leaders are very aware of their organizational cultural and individual differences. They work diligently to ensure that the plans are created in such a way that build on and leverage the collective strengths of the diversity in their organizations. No different than a coach who knows the strengths of her players and manages the team to fully utilize these strengths, leaders who are in tune with the strengths of their teams can effectively motivate and lead them to achieve greatness.

Getting to Organizational Capabilities

Understanding the true organizational capabilities is important for both the overall team as well as the individuals if an organization is to achieve great results. Very often, companies do a fair job of understanding their corporate capabilities. They might even graph their technical competences, competitive advantages, and value-add product differentiators that keep them ahead of others in the marketplace. Organizations are usually able to articulate what they do well and explain why they are better than their competition. However, what few organizations do really well is to have a true understanding of the individual strengths of their team members, beyond their technical or functional expertise. In talent audits, we often capture the individual's technical and business skills and experiences, and even some demographic information about them. We know if they are a person of color and what other languages they speak with some proficiency. Often, that is as deep as we go. We rarely understand the deeper elements of the diversity they bring to the table.

As we discussed in an earlier chapter, there are many ways we can better understand how someone thinks based on their background and experiences. Recall the discussion on the ten value orientations and the associated clusters described by cultural intelligence scholars. Having a picture of whether someone emphasizes individualism versus collectivism, or what their preference is on flexibility versus adaptability as a way to measure their risk tolerance, for instance, would be insightful. Certainly, understanding whether people are more likely to be competitive or collaborative, short-term or long-term focused, or direct or more indirect in their communications preferences is also helpful to getting a complete picture of their overall competencies.

Going beyond this understanding and mapping these individual traits, as well as other qualities, across the individuals in the organization would provide us a whole new appreciation for the true capabilities within our team. Surely that would also inform us of the kinds of behaviors, actions, strategies, and tactics we could utilize to optimize the collective strengths of our team members.

If we are to become great infusion accelerators, we have to be willing to go deeper into the individual strengths of our team. Much like we would measure personality traits and leadership competencies of an individual with tools such as Insights Discovery, we should consider getting a clearer picture of our talent in the organization with a valid cultural intelligence assessment tool that would help generate a baseline understanding of our organizational capabilities. High-CQ leaders understand this insight will put them in a stronger position to drive alignment across people from different backgrounds and ways of thinking.

Step 2: CQ Prism Optics

We define this as "the leader's ability to understand how to leverage the power of the diversity (and all of the differences embodied in this diversity) represented in their organization, and effectively focus them to achieve alignment and forward motion." To gain a full appreciation of what this step entails, we have to understand a bit of the history of diversity and inclusion in the corporate environment.

A Short History of the Evolution of Diversity and Inclusion

On July 26, 1948, President Harry S. Truman signed Executive Order 9981. This executive order abolished discrimination "on the basis of race, color, religion or national origin" in the United States Armed Forces and led to the re-integration of the services during the Korean War. The next day, the headline of the *Chicago Defender* newspaper read "President Truman Wipes Out Segregation in Armed Forces." Ironically, just one or two inches below that headline, there was another headline on the front page of that same paper that read "Posse, Bent on Lynching, Searches Woods for Prey." Clearly, simply writing an executive order was not going to change the hearts and minds of people. It would take much more than just the stroke of a pen.

One could argue that Executive Order 9981, along with US Congress passing the Nineteenth Amendment to the Constitution on June 4, 1919, guaranteeing all American women the right to vote, were the beginning of what today, a hundred years later, is the state of diversity in the United States. Another twenty years would pass after Truman's history executive order, and movements of race equality of the 1960s. During those turbulent years, led by historic and larger-than-life figures like Martin Luther King Jr., the country made some progress in creating a more level playing field for all to enjoy the American dream. Slow progress, but progress nonetheless.

Ever since those early days, we have been inching our way towards creating a more equitable and fair society, where differences of all dimensions are recognized and protected and even leveraged as a collective societal strength. However, it's clear that we still have a very long way to go. Evidence of this fact smacked us all in the face as we witnessed the events unfold over 2020 and 2021 across our nation in places like Chicago, Oregon, and many other cities that were the hotbeds of riots and unrest, often sparked and fueled by race issues. Our people seem deeply divided along some of the same lines of differences that that were headlines of the 1960s. While it would be easy to feel discouraged at what seems to be circular progress, we should take to heart that what has resulted from these historical events is reform in policies and procedures that aim at addressing the root cause of the problem. Again, we have a way to go yet, but the work goes on.

In the corporate environment, whether private or public sectors, and regardless of industry, there has also been progress made in creating more diverse, sensitive organizational cultures. It was back in the early 1970s when Joseph Wilson, CEO of Xerox in New York, along with black employees established National Black Employees Caucus, the first official affinity group (AG). This group aimed at providing a safe environment for difficult topics to be addressed by employees. Ten years later in 1980, Xerox founded the Black Women's Leadership Caucus. Subsequently through the 1980s, affinity groups were created in many companies and ultimately began to evolve into Employee Resource Groups (ERGs). Where affinity groups focused initially on providing a place where people of similar background and experiences could come together to support one another, ERGs recognized the need to go beyond support and began to play a role in career development for its membership. During that time, we saw the formation of many groups focused on women, Hispanics/Latinos, gay and lesbian people, Asians, and others. Along with that, we saw leadership engage, albeit sometimes in words only, in diversity discussions and positions such as chief diversity officer came into vogue at many of the top companies. In the past decades, ERGs have grown to include not only cultural and other identity groups, but also groups based on experiences or interests, such as parenting, volunteerism, wellness, and environmental activism. The natural evolution of ERGs was to form what are now referred to as Business Resource Groups (BRGs), with a focus on leveraging the power of the diversity in the organization and linking them to driving company's revenues and profits, through community outreach.

Most people, including myself, would argue that AGs, ERGs, and BRGs have had a positive influence in organizations. The fact that many reports are issued each year indicating the ranking of companies based on a number of diversity metrics is a good thing. *Fortune* research partner Great Place to Work compiles an annual list of US companies that create inclusive cultures for women and people of all genders, people of color, LGBTQ people, employees who are boomers or older, and people who have disabilities. In addition to diversity numbers, the ranking is based on surveys of employees, who rated the level of camaraderie they experience at work, the effectiveness of their leaders, and other factors that inspire trust in an employer. That's good stuff.

Moreover, we can list many benefits of Employee Resource Groups: They create a great place to grow high-potential leaders, develop community partnerships, assist in attracting diverse talent, and encourage professional development. It is also a place where companies can cultivate mentoring, provide cross-functional teamwork, and offer people at all levels access to senior leadership. There are, however, some disadvantages of Employee Resource Groups. Chief among them are these: Groups can create potential silos within the organization, they can mask issues, and they may create the false impression that diversity issues have been solved. In some cases, having ERGs or BRGs can create more frustration at the grassroots levels when there is no clear progress on issues, and instead leaders are perceived as just lending lip service to the topics of diversity, equity, and inclusion. This is where the high-CQ leader can shine through to take things to the next level. It's leadership's objective to get all the benefits of the diversity in their teams, whether they are organized in ERGs or BRGs or not, while avoiding the disadvantages. That is the sole intent of CQ Prism Optics.

CQ Prism Optics

When I was in third or fourth grade, I first saw my science teacher demonstrate what happens to sunlight when it passes through a prism. It was like watching magic happen. White light on one side of the glass and rainbow of colors on the other. She explained that one way we could easily remember the sequence of colors was to remember the name ROY G. BIV. Red, orange, yellow, green, blue, indigo, and violet. Very cool. That experiment probably help spark my interest even further in science and math. Who knows, she may have been the reason I eventually studied engineering in college.

It was 1666 when Sir Isaac Newton conducted a crucial experiment where he demonstrated that a ray of light is divided into its constituent colors when it is passed through a prism. As an interesting side note, Newton's investigations into optics commenced while he was at his home in Woolsthorpe, Lincolnshire, due to the bubonic plague, which was raging in Cambridge. Given how we have all been rather locked down in our homes as a result of COVID-19 in 2020 and 2021, perhaps many new discoveries have happened from people having more time to experiment, like Sir Isaac Newton did.

Before Newton, it had been thought that color was created by the mixing of light and darkness. Newton noted, however, that the blended print on the white page of a book appears grey, not colored, when viewed from a distance. His experiments in bending light through prisms led to the revolutionary discovery of the existence of a mixture of distinct colored rays distinguishable when white light passed through the prism. That's precisely what we as leaders need to do first: break down our monochromatic teams and understand the rainbow of skills, styles, and ways of thinking (the colors of the individuals in our team) that compose the whole. If you will pardon the intended pun, let's break it down to its parts.

Passing through the First Prism: Separating the Colors

One way to help separate the diversity represented in our organization is through ERGs. We've already discussed the pros and cons of these. In this author's mind, the pros outweigh the cons. ERGs are intended to create a safe, supportive space for employees who share a common identity. An affinity with one another, if you will. They can be effective in providing employees a sense of equity and belonging. The question becomes, which ones do we create? What's their purpose in our organization? How will they be managed? We can list many more questions. Here's the good news: There are many models that work well in terms of creating and implementing ERGs. We don't need to reinvent the wheel. We can learn from other organizations and create a model that will work best for our team. What we need is to keep these principles in mind:

1. Select what ERGs will be encouraged to be formed and implement them uniformly across the organization.
2. Encourage grassroots movements but ensure they are in tune with organizational values and not representative of what might otherwise be considered special interest groups.
3. Provide resources to enable the groups to flourish and be visible within the organization.
4. Allow some autonomy for each ERG to bring its uniqueness forward but ensure they are well aligned with other ERGs in some key aspects of business strategy (more on this later as we discuss harnessing the collective strength).

Leveraging Inclusion

When organizations first began exploring diversity as a concept, the discussions focused mostly on understanding differences between people.

It was important that we raised awareness across the organization to shine a bright light on issues, and the likes and dislikes, of women and people of color. In the early 1990s, when I first joined Johnson & Johnson, the company was just beginning its diversity journey. All managers and leaders, and eventually most employees, were exposed to diversity workshops. These workshops were intended to help us all get in tune with the dimensions of diversity, see how they were represented (or not) in our organization, and equip us with tools needed to effectively communicate across these differences.

Over time, it became clear that awareness was simply not enough. What was needed was inclusion. What was the point of having diverse people in the organization, if they were not included in the decision-making process? Why focus on hiring people of color and increasing our diversity numbers, if we had no real intention of allowing them to have a seat at the table or promoting them in the organization? Inclusion is the point of diversity. To allow all of the team to bring their very best into the organization and truly leverage their skills: that is what we want from diversity.

This then led to the realization that we needed people to feel they belonged in the organization. Now we often hear about diversity, inclusion, and belonging. I am sure there are other words that will be added to the mix over time. However, let's keep it simple. To leverage inclusion in an organization, here are a few things leaders can do:

1. Ensure that managers and leaders are well equipped to have constructive communications with their direct reports. Providing training for all managers to help them become high-CQ individuals is a good start.
2. Ensure that all talent management processes are designed and implemented to maximize the individual strength.

3. Ensure that we have a level playing field for development and promotions.

4. Hold all managers and leaders accountable to walking the diversity and inclusion talk.

5. Proactively encourage and demand full participation. Create a culture that values contributions and seeks to fully utilize the diversity of thought that comes with diversity of people.

6. Keep diversity on the table as a business imperative, with metrics and targets, much like you do other important business drivers.

Passing through the Second Prism: Harnessing the Team's Collective Strength

Perhaps even more significant than his first finding, Newton also showed that the resulting bundle of colored rays that could be seen after passing through the first prism could be reconstituted into white light by a second prism placed in front to the rainbow of colors. This ability to manipulate the light spectrum led to significant scientific advancements that took advantage of the power of breaking a uniform, monochromatic beam of light into a spectrum of color that could be individually manipulated and then brought back together to harness the brightness of a full spectrum. This is precisely what good leaders must be able to do with their teams. They should have the ability to separate the colors and understand the strengths of the individual diversities represented in the team. Second, they need to create the right dynamics in the team that subsequently brings the colors back together to harness the strength of the collective.

To get the team through the second prism, leaders must roll up their sleeves and get to work. This step requires leading the old-fashioned way: from the front. This is what I refer to as "Lieutenant Leadership." In the armed forces, an officer with the rank of lieutenant is a rather junior-level leader. In fact, the first rank we pin on when we are commissioned into the Air Force, Army, or Marines is second lieutenant. A few years later, we are promoted to first lieutenant and change the butter bars (the gold bar insignia indicating their rank) to a silver bar. These officers are often the ones in charge of small units of soldiers and airmen. They are often in the front lines with their troops and take the lead in the forward movement by the troops. The best of these leaders exhibit the following behaviors:

1. *Focus on your people, know your team.* Can anything be more important than knowing as much as we can about those we are privileged to lead? Certainly not. Having your finger on the pulse and being as connected as practical with our people will enable us as leaders to effectively put into practice situational and servant leadership traits that will drive performance.

2. *Focus on alignment rather than agreement.* Oftentimes, teams spend far too much time debating on how to do something trying to get to an agreement, all the while not having focused sufficiently on making sure they are aligned to the mission. We need to make sure there are healthy debates on how something will get done for as long as debates are productive and necessary. We must avoid, however, the analysis paralysis that can occur when team members get lost in the details of tasks or procedural issues and miss the big picture of making sure they are aiming at the same target.

3. *Ensure there is clarity on objectives.* In line with focusing the team on alignment rather than agreement, leaders ensure they have very clearly defined objectives to rally around.

4. *Listen hard and act decisively.* Leaders don't always make the best listeners. So this is a skill that needs to be practiced in order to be perfected. Listening is a very powerful tool, and the leaders who listen best are usually the best ones. However, we must also be willing to act decisively and move the team to action. This means

we must be willing to accept some level of risks and making changes if needed to change course as the team moves forward.

5. *Course correct as often as necessary.* Great leaders are not stubborn. They are, however, persistent. It's the difference between staying on a course of action trying to achieve an objective via brute force, even when the evidence is mounting that the actions are not yielding the desired result, versus staying focused on the end goal and making swift course corrections with the team to achieve the result.

6. *Delegate effectively.* Effective delegation skills are the secret weapon of the good leaders. Good delegation has an empowering effect on the team and the organization as a whole. The corollary of this simple concept (poor delegation) can have devastating consequences and create a culture that stifles creativity and risk taking: the exact opposite of what we want in our teams.

7. *Touch the hearts, not just the minds.* John Maxwell is quoted as having said, "Leaders touch a heart, before asking for a hand." I love that saying. It's a wonderful illustration of two things: first, that leaders work to engage their teams at an emotional level. Second, in the spirit of servant leadership, they ask for a hand. The words here are very important: They ask; they don't demand or extort. What do they ask for? A hand. As in, I have two of my own, but I could use a few more, indicative of leaders who are all in with their teams.

8. *Respect individuality, reward teamwork.* When we respect people and treat them with dignity, valuing not just their contributions, but who they are as a person, we bring out the very best in them. Respecting those we are fortunate to lead is a fundamental principle of a Legacy Leader. In my book, *LEGACYWOMAN: The Legacy Leader as SuperHero*, I outline the principles of leading from the heart; HEART is an acronym that stands for:

- Have a vision
- Empower others
- Act consistently
- Respect your followers
- Take accountability

The "R" is critical to the formula. Equally important, however, is that we reward the collective accomplishments of the team. It's not that we don't recognize individual performance; we do, and we should. However, what must always be kept in focus is the end goal achieved by the team.

Having passed the two prisms with the team, we can now harness their power when we engage them in the vision and together build a road map, a strategy that will lead the organization to success. That's what step 3 is all about. Let's explore that final step next.

Step 3: Fusing/Welding

As the words imply, fusing or welding is the leader's ability to create visions, missions, and strategies that broadly connect individuals (fuses them together) to the bigger purpose and enable them to resonate and align their belief system to that of the organization.

In step 1 of becoming an Infusion Accelerator, leaders considered and gained insight into the individual strengths within their organization. In step 2, they implemented creative ways to promote and enjoy the diversity of groups within the team, while also finding ways to align these groups to work collaboratively to benefit from the strength of the whole. Step 3 is about ensuring that we are creating strategies that leverage the diversity in our organization.

Engaging all members of the team on the journey towards the vision and mission of the organization begins with ensuring it resonates with them. The purpose of the organization must be congruent to them. They must be able to see themselves as a part of the team that will accomplish this ambition. Importantly, they need to feel they fit in, that their contributions are needed and appreciated. They also need to believe the values of the organization are consistent with the vision and mission, and they can connect these values to their own. This is a tall order for any leader. How do we do this? We start with connecting values and strategies with clarity. Next, we enable individuals and teams to have creative license to sculpt the strategy and, to some extent, their roles in it. And third, we bolt these ideas together to drive alignment and action. Let's explore these three ideas further.

Connecting Values and Behaviors to Drive Strategy

Core values describe what's important about your organization's vision and define the behaviors individuals and teams will be held accountable to. I his book *Good to Great*,[8] Jim Collins describes it this way:

> Values define core ideology and culture. They guide innovation and inform a multitude of decisions about how interactions happen, where innovation occurs, and which strategies people choose. Values also help communicate your culture to clients and the team.

Often, when we look at company websites, we find their mission statement and some mention of what their values are. Companies use words to describe their values like integrity, trust, honesty, boldness, accountability, customer focus, passion, and even fun. Facebook lists "be bold, focus on impact, move fast, be open, and build social value" as their five core values.

Procter & Gamble's core values comprise "integrity, leadership, ownership, passion for winning, trust." Johnson & Johnson, a company I proudly served in for nearly eighteen years of my career, is well known for its Credo.

In 1943, Robert Wood Johnson, who was J&J's chairman from 1932 to 1963 and was a member of the company's founding family, crafted the Credo himself. The Credo is the document that clearly spells out the values that guide every decision made in the company. In this incredible document, the needs and well-being of the people the company serves is listed as the first priority. J&J had this philosophy long before anyone ever heard the term "corporate social responsibility." When I first joined the company, I recall being indoctrinated into the Credo as more than just a moral compass. It was indeed presented as a recipe for business success. The longevity and enviable reputation of Johnson & Johnson is the reward the company has enjoyed as a result of living the values spelled out in the Credo. I can tell you from personal experience, the Credo is lived by the leaders at J&J. Behaviors are measured against it. Decisions are guided by it. They are not just words on a wall.

Another company that, like J&J, has a strong foundation of values on which they rely on to operate day to day is Ford Motor Co. Researching Ford, I was intrigued by the way they described their culture. They think of themselves as a family and anchor their culture in shared beliefs and ideals, all acting for the common good. Ford believes that all employees should have the freedom to pursue their dream. This moves them towards maintaining a culture of belonging for every employee. Moreover, Ford has a set of seven behaviors that they refer to as "Our Truths," and they describe these the truths as the guide for how employees at Ford live, act, and communicate.

What are Ford's seven truths? They are: Put people first, Be curious, Build Ford Tough, One Ford, Play to Win, Create Tomorrow, and Do the Right Thing. Further down the page, they define these specifically and describe the expected behaviors by which their team members can go about demonstrating that they are living these truths. In the end, that is what really matters about values. What matters is that the values we state as important lead to behaviors by all members of the team that are consistent with these values.

Having organizational values, of course, is important. However, it is behaviors that really matter most. It may seem obvious, but an important step in establishing a high-performing culture is to clearly define what we expect from our people in their daily behaviors. It is these daily behaviors that truly define the organizational culture. It's not the words we put on the wall, or even the words we say when we are talking about what we value in the company. It is what people see and feel that is actually happening and how people—and leaders in particular—are behaving on a daily basis.

Values are abstract terms. They represent ideas we believe in. Again, it's ideas like integrity, passion, honesty, and teamwork. While values are abstract, behaviors are concrete. They are actions we can see, and sometimes feel, people doing. We can measure behaviors such as

- speaking candidly and transparently at all times,
- holding yourself and other accountable to delivering expectations,
- not playing the blame game,
- focusing on problem solving,
- placing the interest of the team ahead of your own,
- always acting with safety in mind, and
- placing the customer's needs first.

Well-defined behaviors leave very little room for interpretation. You are either acting in ways consistent with those norms, or you're not. Values leave too much room for interpretation. They can mean different things to different people.

As it relates to CQ and being a good infusion accelerator, values can have a very different meaning to people, depending on their cultural background and experiences. A value of respect may be interpreted very differently for someone from a traditional Japanese upbringing and someone from Belgium, for instance. How they may interpret what respect is and how to demonstrate respect are likely as different as night and day. Simply having a value of quality is not sufficient, as the interpretation of what this means and how to exhibit that quality may be different from one person to another, depending on the culture they grew up in. For this reason, we need to focus on clearly articulated behavioral expectations.

Given the diversity of our team, and our understanding of CQ Prism optics, we now know that we have a rainbow of colors associated with the backgrounds, experiences, and skill sets found within the organization. We can appreciate the idea of breaking down the team into its colors (prism 1) and the implication of focusing their collective energy (prism 2). The key to harnessing that energy and getting everyone aligned and collaborating effectively towards the mission is to make sure we are describing our culture in terms of the values we want and the behaviors we expect from our team members. We do that with words and statements that will resonate across the cultural differences. We want our people to not just understand them, but to feel good about them and to embrace them. Ideally, we also want these to be actionable consistently by members of our team, regardless of their individual value system. Clearly, this may not always be possible. There are times when the values held individually by one person, may not be congruent with those of the organization. Sometimes, these differences can be reconciled with a concept referred to as job sculpting. We will cover this in greater detail later in the text.

If the end goal is getting all of our team members to feel connected and in sync with the organizational objectives—and it should be—then we as leaders have to get them to feel inspired by the mission and vision. That is easier said than done. The fact is that most employees are not usually well in tune with their company's purpose. Some data seem to indicate that upwards of 60 percent of employees are not aware of their company's mission statement; even fewer are motivated by it. As much as leaders would like to think that all of their team members have drunk the corporate Kool-Aid, the harsh reality is, there is a high probability a large percentage of their team members are simply not feeling a deep, genuine, and emotional connection with what the company is seeking to achieve. It's more likely that many of their team members feel like just another cog in the wheel.

That does not mean they don't intend on doing a good job or they are not loyal to their work. It does probably mean that we are not getting their A game at all times. So what do we do about this? We must work to connect our people with our purpose. As we have already established, our values define our behaviors, and our behaviors will define our culture. It's our culture that will drive our strategy. Thus, it makes sense that we engage our team as deeply as possible in defining that strategy, making them an integral part of owning it.

There are many ways to go about creating a strategic road map for a company. I've always found that the process is not as important as the engagement with the team that is creating it. To engage people with the process of creating strategy, there are a few key principles leaders should follow:

1. Communicate often and transparently. Always keep the information flowing.

2. Keep the values, behaviors, mission, and vision in the front at all times.

3. Ensure that we are rewarding the right behaviors, dealing with those who are not behaving in accordance with our norms, and hiring to the organizational values and behavior expectations.

4. Create the environment and the opportunity for people to be involved in the process. Listen to people and incorporate their thinking as much as possible.

5. If you have ERGs or BRGs in the organization, purposefully engage them as part of the strategic planning process.

6. Keep the strategy simple.

Creating Room for Creative Sculpting

Another effective way to engage individuals and teams is to make room in the organization for this idea of creative sculpting. In their terrific book *What Motivates Me: Put Your Passions to Work*,[9] Chester Elton and Adrian Gostick introduce this concept of people sculpting their jobs to the extent that this is practical and possible, so they can be fully connected with organization and shape their job to do two things: first, achieve the objectives the company wants and needs, and second, to make the job much more in tune with the individual's passions. This ensures they will put their full energy into the tasks each and every day. Here's what Elton and Gostick say in their book:

> Many people never achieve true happiness and success in their jobs because they don't understand what truly motivates them. In searching for a "dream job", many people feel they have to make a dramatic leap into the unknown. That's usually not the case; in fact, we found the vast majority of people are able to sculpt their current

roles so they can do more of what they love to do and a little less of what they find demotivating.

Such a simple idea, right? But very powerful if you could implement it, essentially giving people permission to redefine (within reasonable limits, of course) elements of their job description or how they deliver on their job description. This has an empowering effect that creates loyalty and alignment with company values and behaviors, while supporting the company's strategic direction. In their book, Elton and Gostick are focused on individuals. However, why not apply these same principles to teams? Why not allow teams to have flexibility in how they define the work they do? Keep in mind that in the end, what we need as leaders is alignment to the end mission and objectives. Agreement on how things get done is only secondary. Thus, creating the environment where individuals and teams can sculpt the how is a great way to ensure they are remaining both aligned and passionate about the work they are doing.

Fusing and welding is not assimilation or a melting pot approach. It's CQ-driven alignment to purpose, building on the collective strengths of the multiple backgrounds represented in the organization to more effectively drive strategy and results.

The Legacy Leader's CQ Accelerator Model provides a clear and actionable framework to enable each of us to take on this journey and achieve a high level of CQ that will be the jet fuel we need to propel ourselves and our teams forward. Engaging everyone in our organization from the top senior levels to the most junior is a powerful way to bring about transformative change in an organization and ensure people are behaving in organically diverse thinking ways. Meaning, when people have a higher level of cultural intelligence, they don't struggle to understand why diversity is important or how they can leverage it to the benefit of all. When you have a team of high-CQ people, they are able to fluidly and naturally communicate with each other, build on their strengths, and collaborate to achieve alignment quicker than other teams. Diversity and inclusion initiatives and actions are no longer just the flavor of the month when you have a high-CQ leader and a high-CQ organization in the mix. Cultural intelligence is not a replacement for the DE&I strategies that companies are working on; it enables them.

High-CQ leaders know they need to create a high-CQ organization so they can influence thinking from the boardroom to the mailroom. They can't do that alone. They need the buy-in, support, and action from executive leadership teams (ELTs) and the board of directors (BOD). Thus, in the next sections of the book, we will explore the roles of ELTs and BODs in driving, leveraging, enabling, and measuring CQ.

PART 3

Enabling CQ Up and Down the Organization

CHAPTER 8

―――――――◆◇◆―――――――

It's Time to Evolve the DE&I Discussion

Thirty years ago, I was fortunate to be recruited by Johnson & Johnson and joined Ethicon, Inc., one of J&J's leading medical device companies. Until that point in my professional career, I had known one employer: the US Air Force. To say that things get done differently in the military as compared to corporate America would be an understatement. Fortunately for me, I had some good coaching by colleagues on "how we do things around here," and I was able to make an effective transition from one organizational culture to another. When I joined Ethicon in 1991, I was the only Latino in Corporate Engineering, based in Somerville, New Jersey. No doubt there were other Hispanics in the organization, predominantly in the production shop floor, but among folks with a manager title or higher, I was a unicorn.

It was around that same time, in the early 1990s, that, with championing by Bob Crocee, then president of Ethicon, the company began a transformative journey in diversity. The company hired a consulting firm focused on diversity, a concept that at that time was early in its entry into Corporate America. With their help, we developed a road map that included creating a high-level strategy along with metrics for diversity, the creation of affinity groups, and training. We had lots and lots of training. It was early in my tenure at Ethicon that I attended my first three-day-long diversity workshop. What I remember most about these workshops is the group discussions. The attendees would be gathered in a circle, and the facilitators would lead a discussion on some topic related to gender or race relations. That was the initial focus of these sessions: helping men and women understand each other better and helping us all understand each other better across race. It was very much primarily a black-and-white race and women-men gender discussion, but eventually over time, it evolved to include Hispanics and Asians. Discussions about gays and lesbians would only come later.

The sessions were rough and emotionally draining. I will admit that at times it felt like the facilitators seem to have an agenda that included getting everyone in the room to have an emotional reaction. They often succeeded. I suppose the idea was to get us all to connect at that emotional level and begin to discuss difficult issues related to our biases and preconceived notions. The intent was good; the initial approach, perhaps, not so much. These workshops did play an important part in creating a foundation for the company and for the diversity movement overall. At least diversity was being talked about and was being included in management discussions. All managers, directors, and vice presidents were required to attend these training sessions, and metrics started to be included in their performance expectations.

Within a few short years, there was an influx of people of color and women into Ethicon as a result of a concerted effort by the company's leadership to diversify the organization's makeup. The workshops continued, and diversity was definitely on the table for discussion. I do recall many conversations with my white male colleagues and my bosses about it. It was clear that they were walking a fine line, awkwardly trying to figure out what to say and what not to say. What should they do, and how should they behave? It was also clear that they felt singled out as the bad guys in a movie.

Perhaps some of you, as you read this, are thinking, *This is what is happening in my company now.* Or perhaps others are wondering out loud, "Why hasn't much changed in the past thirty years?" It's not hard to feel that way. All we need to do is look at the current state of our social environment. During the COVID years, 2020 and 2021, we saw unrest across the United States at levels that have not been seen since the 1960s. We saw the rise of movements such as Me Too and Black Lives Matter. We have continued to hear the outrage over social injustices done to people of color, Asians, and others. In corporate America, leaders huddle to try to determine the best way to respond to these dynamics, while continuing to keep focused on their business imperatives. They wonder how they should respond to these different social forces, or even if they should respond at all.

Now before we get too far down the road and start to think in overly pessimistic ways, and tunnel down the rabbit hole of despair and hopelessness, we should remember the following important fact: We have come a very long way, both in the corporate environment and in society at large, relative to diversity. Diversity and all of its dimensions is more readily accepted today, and most organizations have engaged in their own journey of figuring out how to leverage differences in their teams. Of course, there is work yet to be done. Personally, I am optimistic that we will see the needle move much faster in the coming years, than we have in the past couple of decades. The engineer in me processes problems in logical thinking ways. Engineers tend to first understand the problem (i.e., the current state), figure out the root cause, and then engineer solutions. Let's apply that thinking process to the issue of diversity, and based on what the current state is, try to determine the root causes and finally come up with a few ways we can improve the process going forward.

Today's State of Diversity in the Corporate Environment

For our purposes in this book, we are going to use the US workforce as the basis for analysis and understanding. I believe it is fair to say that while the diversity dynamics can be different from one region of the world to the next, the general principles will be the same. To state it bluntly, the US workforce has a diversity problem, especially at the executive level. Yes, we have already acknowledged that progress has been made over the past few decades; however, the data are still overwhelming that the number in terms of representation of diverse people at all levels of management and leadership in organizations lags well behind the reported population demographics by race, gender, and other differences.

Here is just one set of data to support the point above: according to the latest US census report, Hispanics/Latinos make up 18 percent of the US population, yet less than 7 percent of Congress members are Latino. Fewer than 3 percent of Fortune 1000 company board seats are held by Latinos, and in fact, 65 percent of the top thousand companies in America don't even have one Latino on their board. Less than 5 percent of the top CEOs in the US are Latino. Women, although there has been significant progress made in the recent years, still represent less than 30 percent of board seats in the S&P 500 companies and only 8 percent of Fortune 500 CEOs. Significantly, today still about 90 percent of Fortune 500 CEOs are white males. We have a long way to go.

It is interesting to also look at what happened to diversity as a subject of corporate discussion over the past fifteen years. During the 1990s, diversity was the topic of the decade. Most large companies began establishing diversity programs, appointing the newly created positions of chief diversity officer, and the title of diversity manager came into vogue. Affinity groups (later known as Employee Resource Groups) were being formed with the support and sponsorship of executive leaders, and they were being well funded. Nonprofit organizations focused on professional development for people of color were also being well supported financially by companies. Organizations such as the National Society of Hispanic MBAs (now known as PROSPANICA), the Association of Latino Professionals for America (ALPFA), and many others were having successful recruiting and job fairs and conventions, and their membership numbers swelled quickly. Then a financial crisis hit in the late 1990s. Diversity, like many other programs, began to experience cutbacks in funding and strategic focus.

A decade passed, and we saw a definitive decline in importance that leadership teams were placing on diversity. It was different, and suddenly we started to experience what I describe as diversity fatigue. The ERGs and professional organizations struggled to get attention. People of color who had been hired by companies were first to be laid off because companies were having to right-size their organizations. Since people of color were the more junior folks, they were often the ones let go to the benefit of those with more seniority. Here we are in 2022, and diversity is back on the table with a renewed vigor, likely as a result of what is going on socially in the world and because perhaps leaders at the senior most levels of the organization have come to believe that diverse organizations perform better than nondiverse teams. The good news is that we are back discussing it and making diversity a strategic imperative again. What is important is making sure we move the dialogue forward to learn from past mistakes and create sustainable approaches to ensuring diversity is not a program or fad, but a way of thinking and working that becomes a part of the organization's DNA.

Why Haven't Some DE&I Programs Succeeded?

If we are to figure out how to evolve the discussion to truly create effective, diverse, and inclusive organizational cultures, it's important we have some reference of what has not worked thus far. The primary reason that diversity and inclusion programs don't work is because there is no clear leadership call to action and accountability for change. It's no different than any other strategic imperative or initiative; if there is no leadership mandate, with clear expectations and metrics, it simply will not get done. Importantly as leaders, we must get specific on the behaviors we expect from our team members.

The reasons we have so much diversity fatigue is that what organizations, and their leaders, do around DE&I is often superficial and perceived as all talk. Moreover, that fatigue leads to people of color being frustrated and feeling disenfranchised. That is probably the worst unintended consequence of just talking diversity as opposed to really walking it each day.

In her March 2021 *Forbes EQ* article for the National Diversity Council,[10] Erika Johnson, managing partner and cofounder of Next Wave Strategies, wrote this:

> Many organizations face a moment of cultural reckoning from the lack of centering diversity and inclusion programs in the past. While D&I programs strive to influence participation and representation in diverse groups, poor implementation can adversely affect adaptation success.

Johnson goes on to describe the top four reasons implemented DE&I programs fail. These programs fail because the company does not have a long-range plan relative to diversity, they lack commitment to the program, they have poor instructional delivery models, and they lack diversity representation. Fundamentally, I agree with these four reasons. However, I think the sequence of how we think about it matters. In my view, the reasons why DE&I programs have not been as effective as possible are the following:

1. *Missing DE&I as a strategic business imperative in the long-range plan.* Diversity is not a program or an initiative. It must be a way of thinking and operating. Leaders must integrate the values of a diverse and inclusive culture with organizational objectives. In fact, if DE&I is not listed as a business imperative and included in the strategic road map, then it will not get the leadership attention it requires to be effectively integrated into the everyday way that work gets done. Moreover, if the DE&I imperative is not aligned to the organizational strategic plan, there is very low probability that any progress achieved will be sustained in the long term. Johnson refers to DE&I as a program. It must not be thought of as a program. Programs have a beginning and an end. They are subject to the whims of economic conditions affecting a business. Like travel expenses and other controllable expenses, if DE&I programs are cut from the budget when things get financially tight for the company, then it's not really a business imperative. DE&I must be perceived and felt by all as a nonnegotiable. It is a business driver, with key deliverables and specific metrics, and with clear, unequivocal accountability at all leadership levels. If DE&I has failed in some organizations, we need only look to the leadership's commitment as the root cause.

2. *Leaders not modeling the right behaviors*: Chapter 6 discussed the importance of leaders modeling the right behaviors to encourage a high-CQ culture. Simply put, leaders must model DE&I principles. If they don't, why would others take it on? When employees sense a lack of commitment to diversity, and they see no accountability for the folks above them, they are quick to disengage from the process themselves. No leadership modeling equals no organic DE&I thinking throughout the organization.

3. *Lack of or inconsistent training on CQ and DE&I*: Cultural intelligence enables organic DE&I thinking at all organizational

levels. Please read that last sentence again. If you remember nothing else after reading this book, please remember that.

From 1991 to 1997, I was assigned as a social actions officer at McGuire Air Force Base in New Jersey. I was a captain at the time, and my responsibilities included developing a sexual harassment training program that would be required for all base personnel. I recall standing before the troops, many of them very young, and educating them on the military's policy regarding sexual harassment. We also covered the impact on troop effectiveness and morale when some felt victim of harassment. I also recall making this provocative statement: "I don't care how you think about sexual harassment or discrimination; I care how you act." What I meant in saying that was this: "Perhaps I can't change the way you think about something, but I surely can and will hold you accountable as to how to behave."

I suppose at the time, I did not think it was practical to believe you could change how some think or feel. Over time, I have come to change that position. I do believe we can rewrite the hardwired code in our DNA that defines how we think about those who are different from us. I believe that if we confront our innermost, unconscious biases and learn to deal with them effectively, we can modify our behaviors to be more naturally inclusive.

When it comes to DE&I training, perhaps the reasons they have not been effective is because the focus has been on the mechanics of behavior. We have focused on teaching people how they should behave towards certain "others," and in some cases, that has created more of an awkward, walking-on-eggshells environment than a collaborative one. Behaviors are important; we have already established that. However, what we want is people to be their authentic selves, while at the same time having an appreciation of where they come from, how they show up, and how they most effectively interact with those who are different from them. That starts with CQ training. Thus, if we want to enable a true DE&I culture, what we really need to do is help people get on their own journey to driving their CQ index higher. Higher CQ people think in organic DE&I ways. That is the end game: Get folks thinking in inclusive ways as the normal way of doing things.

4. *Lack of inclusion and representation*: In her article, Johnson explains that everyone must have a seat at the table and that a DE&I program cannot succeed in the absence of adequate representation of diverse groups of people. Moreover, she explains that a key hindrance is the perception of diversity as anything other than meaning the inclusion of people of all sorts of differences, including gender, ethnicity, and many other dimensions. She concludes that many DE&I programs fail because of the lack of appropriate representation and inclusion of diverse groups.

She's exactly right. If folks are not really included and represented, it becomes obvious in the organization. Equally important, it becomes obvious to those outside the company. In today's talent war environment, recruiting has become increasingly complex. With the availability of information about companies via social media outlets beyond just their own websites, prospective employees can learn a lot about their potential employer before making the decision to join them or not. If they look at the company and see a gap in representation of people who look like them at all organizational levels, they think twice about joining. After all, what chances will they have for advancement and professional development if the inclusion stops at the junior levels of the company?

5. *Ironically, DE&I initiatives have not been inclusive and in some cases have created silos.* Historically, diversity initiatives in companies has meant there would be a focus on hiring people of color and women, and ERGs were created to provide a place for them to feel supported. In the more advanced organizations, there would be a concerted effort to make sure developmental opportunities became available to women and people of color. We promoted women and people of color to slowly, but surely, change the configurations of management and leadership teams to be more diverse. This is all good stuff. I, for one, applaud companies that continue to do this. However, this emphasis can sometimes have unintended consequences. What happens to a group that suddenly feels marginalized, set apart, or left out? What about the white males, for instance? We know that some have felt that because of DE&I initiatives in their organizations, they may not have had the opportunity or promotion that went to another. Is that fair? The short answer is no, that's not fair. The reality is, there is simply no way to favor one group without impacting another. Some would say, "The white male had an advantage for all the years before." This is true. But what does this have to do with the white male who is in the workplace now and trying to make his way, the same as everyone else? You see the problem? There is no perfect answer. Trying to fix it going forward by forcing the disadvantage of one group over another is a less than ideal solution. In fact, it creates more problems than it solves.

    The silos created by having ERGs of all types that work as little groupings and in isolation from one another is also, to some degree, a part of the problem. Then, what's the answer? The answer, albeit an imperfect one, is this: It's up to the leaders to make sure we create a culture where all can truly be engaged, valued, and included. That we work to enable all in the organization to become high-CQ people, and then using the principles of an infusion accelerator, we harness the individual's power to the benefit of all. In this case, consider CQ as the great equalizer. You see, CQ applies to everyone. No matter your race, color, or creed, we can each take a CQ journey and become better collaborators and team members.

Let's conclude this chapter on a high note. There has been a resurgence of emphasis on DE&I across the globe and certainly within the corporate world, in both private and public sectors. Boards of directors and senior leaders are asking the question: how do we take this to the next level? They want to know how they can ensure that diversity and inclusion is not just something that is talked about, but that it is truly leveraged up and down their organization for maximum effectiveness. The answer has to include the following steps: make DE&I a business imperative and treat it as any other key business driver, focus on the top ten DE&I imperatives (to be discussed in chapter 9), enable the journey to high CQ for all in the organization, ensure that there is full commitment at the top, and insist that the tone from the top is consistent with the values and behaviors expected of all.

In the previous chapters, we dealt with enabling the leader's CQ journey, and later in this book, we will address how we can gain commitment and action at the board and executive levels of the organization to drive cultural intelligence from the mailroom to the boardroom. There is one more important topic that we must address so we can move from the idea that "It's time to evolve the DE&I discussion" to actually doing it. In order to truly drive the DE&I discussion forward and fundamentally alter how we work, we must do two things: create a foundation based on Culturally Intelligent leaders and individuals throughout an organization, and ensure we have a strategy that is focused on what I call the top ten DE&I imperatives. Let's get after these top ten imperatives in chapter 9.

CHAPTER 9

The Top Ten DE&I Imperatives

Eight billion dollars: That is what some estimate American companies spend annually on diversity training and programs. The cost just to create and implement a comprehensive DE&I program can range from $25,000 to $450,000. The amazing thing is that companies have been spending this money on DE&I each year, even though they have remarkably few results. That raises a very important question: Why do it? I am a business-minded person. I believe I've been effective in running many companies over the years. I've helped make them more financially successful than when I first took the reins. One thing is sure: We (myself and the teams I was privileged to lead) did not invest in things that were not shown to work. Most of the decisions we make in companies have a financial consideration. Therefore, we must think of DE&I initiatives in the same way we do other business investments. If the return on investment on projects and initiatives is not proven over time, companies stop investing in them. It's a simple good business principle and practice. That leaves us with a very important question: If DE&I programs have not yielded good results, then why do them at all?

The first step in finding an answer to a problem is making sure we are asking the right question. The question of "Why have DE&I programs if they don't yield results?" is a rhetorical one. Its basic premise is that DE&I

programs don't work. The problem is that the data don't support that premise. The facts indicate that investing in diversity creates more effective teams that outperform monolithic ones. In the for-profit business world, that translates to making more money.

In the 1990s and early part of 2000s, many financial companies were settling high-profile sex-discrimination lawsuits. Morgan Stanley paid out $54 million. Merrill Lynch dished out more than $100 million. In 2007, Morgan paid another $46 million to settle a class action suit, and in 2013, Bank of America Merrill Lynch settled a race discrimination suit for $160 million. These are just a few visible examples of the financial pain companies suffered as a result of bad practices related to diversity issues. The point is that companies started to care, because it was hitting them in the wallet. In the early 1990s, this led to the diversity movement in corporate America. As a result of the financial hit these giant companies were absorbing, it's not surprising that they made adjustments. They implemented diversity training programs and revamped their recruiting and promotion policies. Interestingly, they also added a rule that all new hires sign arbitration contracts, agreeing not to join class actions suits; I suppose it was a hedge against the diversity programs not working.

Despite all of this work, things have not changed much over the past few decades. Although the proportion of Latino managers at US commercial banks rose from 4.5 percent in 2003 to 5.7 percent in 2014, white women's representation dropped from 39 percent to 35 percent, and black men's representation dropped slightly from 2.5 percent to 2.3 percent. From 1985 to 2014, among all US companies with a hundred or more employees, the proportion of black men in management increased just slightly from 3 percent to 3.3 percent. It seems I am making an argument against spending on diversity, because it did not help much, at least in this example. However, there is more to the story.

In January 2015, Vivian Hunt, Dennis Layton, and Sara Prince of McKinsey & Co., published "Why Diversity Matters."[11] Their opening paragraph says it all:

> We know intuitively that diversity matters. It's also increasingly clear that it makes sense in purely business terms. Our latest research finds that companies in the top quartile for gender or racial and ethnic diversity are more likely to have financial returns above their national industry medians. Companies in the bottom quartile in these dimensions are statistically less likely to achieve above-average returns. And diversity is probably a competitive differentiator that shifts market share toward more diverse companies over time.

As part of their research, Hunt, Layton, and Prince examined proprietary data sets for 366 public companies across a range of industries in Canada, Latin America, the United Kingdom, and the United States. They looked at financial results and the composition of top management and boards. The findings were significant. According to their study, companies in the top quartile for gender-diverse executives were 15 percent more likely to generate above-average profitability compared to the bottom quartile of companies, whose executive teams were predominantly white and male. Related to staffing, companies that have higher degrees of racially and ethnically diverse employees have a 35 percent performance advantage over companies relying on a culture fit that trends to white and monocultural.

They also reported that companies with gender-diverse executive teams in the highest quartile outperformed male-dominated companies by 21 percent in terms of earnings and 27 percent in terms of creating long-term value. Racially diverse executive teams yielded 35 percent higher earnings before interest and taxes (EBIT) and 33 percent more long-term value creation over the least racially diverse companies.

Perhaps most importantly, companies with diverse talent and executives are shown to be more likely to retain the best talent. In today's talent war climate, where attrition rates are at all-time highs, and we are dealing with what some are referring to as the Great Resignation (that is, employees voluntarily quitting their jobs in record numbers), being able to attract and retain talent is a key and significant business driver. With millennials and Gen-Z becoming the dominant generation in the workforce, attracting young talent must take diversity into account, given that they are the most diverse generation in history.

Hunt, Layton, and Prince close their article with a very important conclusion. They suggest that given the higher returns that diversity is expected to bring, it is better for organizations to invest earlier rather than later because "winners will pull further ahead, and laggards will fall further behind." There's not much left to doubt, relative to the value of diversity to companies. Thus, the question "Why do it?" has an obvious and simple response: We do it because it works, and it makes organizations more attractive, effective, and profitable. Period. Therefore, the question is not "Why do it?" The correct question is, "Why hasn't it worked?"

In August 2016, Frank Dobbin and Alexandra Kalev wrote "Why Diversity Programs Fail" for the *Harvard Business Review*.[12] In their article, they write:

> It shouldn't be surprising that most diversity programs aren't increasing diversity. Despite a few new bells and whistles, courtesy of big data, companies are basically doubling down on the same approaches they've used since the 1960s—which often make things worse, not better.

Firms have long relied on diversity training to reduce bias on the job, hiring tests and performance ratings to limit it in recruitment and promotions, and grievance systems to give employees a way to challenge managers. Those tools are designed to preempt lawsuits by policing managers' thoughts and actions. Yet laboratory studies show that this kind of force-feeding can activate bias rather than stamp it out. As social scientists have found, people often rebel against rules to assert their autonomy. Try to coerce me to do X, Y, or Z, and I'll do the opposite just to prove that I'm my own person.

And there it is. The answer to the question "Why hasn't it worked?" We continue to do the same thing over again and expect a different result. That's also the perfect definition of insanity.

Dobbin and Kalev go on to write:

In analyzing three decades' worth of data from more than 800 U.S. firms and interviewing hundreds of line managers and executives at length, we've seen that companies get better results when they ease up on the control tactics. It's more effective to engage managers in solving the problem, increase their on-the-job contact with female and minority workers, and promote social accountability—the desire to look fair-minded. That's why interventions such as targeted college recruitment, mentoring programs, self-managed teams, and task forces have boosted diversity in businesses. Some of the most effective solutions aren't even designed with diversity in mind.

The most significant sentence in that paragraph is the last one: "Some of the most effective solutions aren't even designed with diversity in mind." Let's start there. Now that we've asked the right question, and we know the answer, we should consider what has been done that hasn't worked and do something different.

Here's a short list of a few things that have been tried and have not really worked well:

1. *Legislating behavior expectations.* You just can't tell people how to behave and expect that they will blindly abandon all their biases (implicit and explicit).

2. *Diversity training*: Despite the fact that nearly half of smaller to midsize companies do it, and all Fortune 500 companies do it, the positive effects of diversity training rarely last beyond a day or two, and a number of studies suggest that it can activate bias or spark a backlash.

3. *Creating quotas for recruiting and promoting people of color.* What we have seen is more of a revolving door when it comes to people of color being recruited to a company. They arrive and often leave for other opportunities in a short period of time. Promoting anyone for any reason other than their competence, expertise, and the value they can add is simply bad business.

4. *Celebrating special interest groups* during a specific month of the year with social gatherings, invited speakers, and picnics or other company functions.

5. *Creating Employee Resource Groups (ERGs) or Business Resource Groups (BRGs)* without a specific charter mission or true leadership sponsorship and accountability.

Let's be perfectly clear on this next point: Doing the above-mentioned items that are normally and routinely done by organizations aiming to have a positive impact on diversity, equity, and inclusion is not a bad thing. We do want to legislate behaviors; that is, we need policies and rules in place to institutionalize the standards of behaviors that we expect of our employees. We do want to do training; we just need to make sure it's the appropriate training and current to the issues of the day. We want to make sure to have checks and balances on recruiting and promoting practices to enable diverse slates to be considered. Of course, we should celebrate Hispanic Awareness Month, Black History Month, LGBTQ Pride Month, Women's History Month, Asian Pacific Heritage Month, and others. Why not? However, if that is all we do, then we are missing the mark. Finally, BRGs and ERGs can be very powerful instruments for a company to leverage its diversity and empower its people. Thus, it's not that these things are wrong; it's more likely we are not implementing them correctly with the right focus and links to the organizational strategy.

Over the past thirty years, I have seen the ups and downs and ebbs and flows of diversity as a topic of discussion in the corporate setting. We have all experienced the recent resurgence of the topic and the rebirth of DE&I as a business imperative. However, if programs lack foresight, inclusivity, and a commitment from organizational leaders, sustainable change is unlikely. To achieve sustainability and enable organizations to think in what I like to refer to as "organically diverse" ways, we need three things: First, we need executive leadership ownership and accountability. Second, we need to build a foundation based on the cultural intelligence of everyone in the organization. Finally, we need to develop and implement programs that build on this foundation and avoid some of the natural resistance and fatigue that comes along with diversity programs. On this last point, there are ten imperatives that, as leaders, we need to consider as we develop strategies to impact culture in a sustainable way. They will be critical to creating organizations that have a diverse mindset and modus operandi that is part of the fabric, the DNA, of the teams they lead.

Imperative 1. Don't Drive Diversity Awareness; Drive Inclusion

In the early 1990s, when diversity training was first being introduced in a significant way to corporate America's Fortune 100 companies, the focus was awareness. The goal was simply to make us each aware of the differences between people. In fact, the focus was often restricted (and sadly, it still is, in many ways) to a gender (man and woman) and race (black and white) discussion. The many other dimensions of diversity were largely overlooked and did not even become a part of the dialogue until later in the 2000s.

As we have already discussed, Business Resource Groups and Employee Resource Groups were initially referred to as affinity groups (AGs). As that name implies, it was about creating a safe place where people with similar affinities could come together to support and enable each other. Groups were formed around shared interests or common goals to which individuals could belong. The initial focus was about making others aware of what it meant to be from that group; whether it was about understanding what Hispanics are like, or what the gay community is like, or how women think or want to be treated. In hindsight, it almost seems trivial and perhaps even naïve to think that groups needed to be formed for this reason. However, they were, and they served a good purpose. Awareness of differences became a good starting place from which we could learn how to better collaborate with each other across these differences.

Over time, it became evident that while awareness is a nice thing to have, it fell short of helping create a truly diverse organization. The true purpose is to leverage the skills of all, regardless of differences, to achieve accelerated and improved results. For that to happen, the diverse people we have in the organization need to be included in the process. People need to feel that their input is heard and valued, and that their contributions are sought out and considered as part of the decision-making process. Inclusion is the key, not awareness. Yet our strategies, the activities we promote under the diversity banner, and even the way we treat people of color in our organizations often focus more on making us aware of the differences as opposed to helping us leverage the strength of the collective by ensuring we are acting in inclusive ways. If inclusion is the key to leveraging diversity, cultural intelligence is the enabler of individuals thinking in inclusive ways. High-CQ individuals and high-CQ organizations are naturally inclusive.

How can leaders test to see if their strategies focus on inclusion rather than awareness? Here are a few simple questions to consider:

o   Are we educating leaders to become culturally intelligent?
o   Have we committed publicly to leveraging everyone on the team?
o   How are we actively listening to our people?
o   How are we encouraging innovative thinking?

Imperative 2. Don't Recruit Diverse Talent; Attract Them

In the past few years, and specifically since 2020, when COVID changed how we work forever, the talent market has seen a tectonic shift the likes of which we have not seen before. While the stock and housing markets, and other economic industries, have also seen some radical changes, it's fair to say they have been dwarfed by what has happened in the job market. With unprecedented levels of layoffs around the globe at the beginning and during the middle of the COVID pandemic, to the dramatic shift in people voluntarily leaving their positions towards the later parts of the pandemic, the way people work and, more importantly, the way they want to work has been transformed in less than twenty-four months. Most experts agree that it will never be the same again. People are now making decisions on what they want to do, how they want to do it, and who they want to do it for based on an entirely new set of rules.

What has become clear is that for those who can, they are making decisions about work that are based primarily on personal and family reasons, including spending more time at home, living where they want to rather than where the job might be, and how they feel about the company they are working for, rather than the economic considerations of salary or benefits. The shift to work from home, first forced by the COVID pandemic, has resulted in a new paradigm with people now being reluctant to return to the office. Additionally, in the United States, stimulus checks, unemployment benefits, and vaccinations (or lack thereof) paved the way for many Americans who had been feeling burned out to take a break and consider new ways of living and working.

One way this has manifest is in the turnover tsunami that companies in all sectors have seen. In 2022, one company I worked with experienced more than 50 percent attrition. That level of turnover can create havoc in an organization, and although a good leadership team can take advantage of this level of staff change to make necessary and transformative change in the organizational structure, focus, and even culture, the disruption to the business can be severe. In most cases, this level of attrition has a negative impact on the company results for the short and long term. The worst may yet be to come. Some experts estimate that more than 50 percent of workers plan on looking for new jobs in the next twelve months. The cost of this turnover is high. Consider the expensive processes behind recruiting, hiring, and training, not to mention the time spent on onboarding a new team member. Moreover, when an employee leaves, the company suffers a lack of continuity, loss of momentum in some cases, and negative client impact, not to mention the loss of intellectual capital. These costs are hard to measure in financial terms, but their impact is profound to a company.

Given this shift in how the world now works, and the ability for people to be quite selective in how they work, when they work, where they work, and who they work for, how should organizations go about getting the talent they need when there is competition for the best of the best from organizations across the globe? Can we simply double down on our efforts to recruit? Should we just offer more pay and benefits than the competition? Do we let everyone set their own terms and work conditions? Are we willing to overlook culture and values fit with candidates simply because they are scarce, and we just need people? This can't possibly be the answer, and it certainly is not sustainable. Organizations need to shift their strategy from recruiting to attracting talent.

Is there a difference between recruiting talented people and attracting them? In this author's viewpoint, the difference is like night and day. Recruitment is the process of actively seeking out, finding, and hiring candidates for a specific position or job. The key action here is "actively seeking out." This translates to finding these talented resources where they currently are and convincing them to look at you as an alternative. Attracting talent, on the other hand, is quite different. Look at the definition of the word *attracting*: "cause to come to a place or participate in a venture by offering something of interest, favorable conditions, or opportunities." Synonyms for the word *attract* include "allure," "captivate," "charm," "enchant," and "fascinate." To state the obvious, the difference between recruiting and attracting is who looks for whom. When you are recruiting, you're doing the looking. When you are attracting, they are looking for you.

Another way to think about it is this: Organizations need to focus their strategies on having a culture that attracts people. They should think about how to become talent magnets. Then their recruiting practices will be much more effective, as people will be lining up wanting to be included in the interviewing process.

High-performing talent ask themselves these questions when deciding whether to join a team or not:

- o What is the reputation of the leaders in the company?
- o What's the culture of this organization? What do current and former employees say about it? What do customers say about it?
- o Is this company known as a place where people are respected, valued, and developed?
- o Does this organization have a good reputation and obvious concern for social impact issues?
- o Do I see myself represented in this company? Are there others like me? How are they doing in the company?

Here are some questions companies can ask to test their strategies and ensure they are talent magnets focused on attracting, rather than simply recruiting, talent:

- o Are leaders involved in the process of attracting talent?
- o Are we committed to a talent audit process?
- o How do we measure organizational pride? How are we building a culture of accountability and commitment?
- o How are we involving an employee's family or support networks?
- o How are we measuring the effectiveness of our social media strategy and our brand reputation?

Leaders must ensure that their organizational culture is such that it becomes a talent magnet for high-caliber talent. Recruiting is relatively easy. You go where the talent is, offer them a very competitive compensation and benefits package, and provide them a flexible work environment that meets their needs, and you'll probably get them to come work for you. How long they stay with you, well, that's a different problem, and it leads us to the next diversity imperative.

Imperative 3. Don't Just Retain Diverse Talent; Develop and Challenge Them

You may be picking up on the theme here that these imperative statements are intended to be provocative. Some reading this might be thinking, *Wait, first you tell me I shouldn't focus on recruiting talent, and now I shouldn't care about retaining them, either?* Setting humor aside for a moment, of course, we care about recruiting talent. As we indicated in our discussion on Imperative 1, it's important that we focus on creating an attractive environment for talent, and that will enable our recruiting. It's about having the priorities in the right order. Similarly, here we should not focus on retaining people. Rather, we should spend our effort in ensuring that once we have the talent onboard, we are investing in their development, personal and professional, and challenging them to grow and contribute in increasingly significant ways. The question now is, how do we move from the Great Resignation to the Great Retention?

In his 2017 McKinsey & Co. article, "Attracting and Retaining the Right Talent,"[13] Scott Keller wrote this:

> Since business leaders know that talent is valuable and scarce, you might assume that they would know how to find it. Not so. A whopping 82 percent of companies don't believe they recruit highly talented people. For companies that do, only 7 percent think they can keep it. More alarmingly, only 23 percent of managers and senior executives active on talent-related topics believe their current acquisition and retention strategies will work. These leaders aren't being humble—most companies just aren't good at this stuff. Gallup reported that in a 2015 survey, more than 50 percent of respondents were "not engaged"; an additional 17.2 percent were "actively

disengaged." Related surveys report that 73 percent of employees are "thinking about another job" and that 43 percent were more likely to consider a new one than they had been a year earlier.

Those are some rather significant statistics. He goes on to write:

> The fact that the Baby Boomers' decades of knowledge and experience are now leaving the workplace forever makes this state of play more unsettling. At the natural-resources giant BP, for example, many of the most senior engineers are called "machine whisperers" because they can keep important, expensive, and temperamental equipment online. If high-quality talent isn't brought in to replace such people, the results could be catastrophic.

> And the scarcer top talent becomes, the more companies that aren't on their game will find their best people cherry-picked by companies that are. In future, this will be even more likely, since millennials are far less loyal to their employers than their parents were. The Bureau of Labor Statistics says that workers now stay at each job, on average, for 4.4 years, but the average expected tenure of the youngest workers is about half that.

The bottom line is very clear: Retention is a business imperative. Turnover is costly, disruptive, and damaging to the organizational culture. The keys to retention can be as simple as taking care of three basic principles best captured in April 2022 by Roger Martin in his *Harvard Business Review* article, "The Real Secret to Retaining Talent. The Subtle Art of Making People Feel Special."[14] In his article, Martin boiled it down to three simple yet profound ideas in terms of how we manage people:

1. Never dismiss their ideas
2. Never block their development
3. Never pass up the chance to praise them

I would have added a fourth idea to Martin's; namely, never stop being socially conscious and accountable.

Here's my interpretation of his three principles: First, to retain people, you must always show them respect. That's the principle of never dismissing their ideas. It also means people will feel included. As we have already emphasized, this is the point of diversity in the first place. Second, always put people's development first. The more you invest in them, the more likely they will feel some allegiance to the team. Block them from developing, however, and you are sure to lose them. Third, never underestimate the power of "thank you" and other forms of appropriate praise. Finally, adding my idea to Martin's three, people, especially the younger generations of today, are much more socially conscious and active, and they want to feel like they are working with organizations that have a larger purpose than simply the art of making money.

Here are a few questions leaders can ask to test whether the organization is focused on retaining talent:

o   Are we investing in a transformative learning culture?
o   Are we living up to our corporate social responsibility and environmental impact focus?
o   Do we have sustainable processes to support talent development?
o   How are we reinforcing and living organizational values?

Imperative 4. Don't Promote Diversity; Ensure a Level Playing Field for Promotions

Try this simple exercise: take a moment to think about the top three to five criteria by which you think promotions should be determined. When I do that exercise and think about the reasons why someone should be promoted, here's what I come up with:

- o   Performance: They have done a great job and consistently meet or exceed job expectations.
- o   Accountability: They are accountable for their actions, and more than this, they take initiative in their areas of responsibility.
- o   Attitude: They have a positive attitude and demonstrate a can-do behavior consistently.
- o   Leadership: They are recognized by others as a key contributor, a go-to person, and even a thought leader in their areas of expertise.
- o   Innovation: They have an innate curiosity, are creative, and are innovative thinkers.
- o   Self-directed: They are able to manage themselves and their responsibilities with little or no direction.
- o   Readiness: They are clearly ready and deserving of the next organizational level, the recognition and the reward that go along with that.
- o   Skill sets: They have the necessary skills (or potential to develop them) for the position they are being promoted to.

In my research on criteria for employee promotions, I found many good resources with a variety of reasons why people should get promoted. With very few exceptions, the lists were similar, and in nearly no examples that I found was there mention of promoting someone based on diversity (i.e., because the person was from any particular group). No one wants to get promoted based on the color of their skin, gender, sexual orientation, or any other nonperformance-related metric. The leader's role here is quite simple. They need to make certain the playing field is level, that all who are qualified are considered and measured against the same bar, and that policies and procedures are in place to make sure the process protects fairness.

Clearly, we have to ensure that promotion slates, just like recruiting slates, are diverse. Surely and, regrettably, still, we do have to track organizational performance against some metrics regarding the diversity of our employee population and the rates of promotions for diverse groups of people. If we find these to be lacking, then we must go back to the drawing board of our organizational culture and our policies to find the root cause. It would be easy to blame it on a few managers and leaders, who allow their unconscious bias to get the best of them and continue to perpetuate the idea of promoting that which we are comfortable with. No doubt, they should be held accountable for that track record. However, if we are going to systematically root out the problem, we must deal with both the individuals who are not truly and organically thinking with a culturally intelligent mindset and the policies and procedures that allow it to occur.

Here are some questions leaders can ask to test whether the organization has a level playing field relative to promotions:

- o   How do we focus on culture and inclusion?
- o   How are we using our succession planning process?
- o   Are we following a performance and talent development system?
- o   Are we holding managers accountable to manage performance and their individual track records of people development?

Imperative 5. Don't Just Celebrate Diversity; Respect It

I love the idea of celebrating diversity. I don't mean just literally in the party way, although there is nothing wrong with that idea. For instance, I always appreciate the special events that we enjoy around Hispanic Awareness Month. We celebrate our heritage with great food, good music, and some other traditions that can be so much fun. However, to celebrate diversity really means understanding and appreciating the uniqueness of each individual and groups of people and recognizing these individual differences. Whatever dimensions these differences are (race, ethnicity, gender, sexual orientation, age, physical abilities, socioeconomic status, religious or political beliefs, or other ideologies), if we want to create an inclusive environment in our workplaces, as well as in our communities, we must really go beyond celebrating diversity, and we must truly respect diversity.

There are several definitions for the word *respect*. One of them is "due regard for the feelings, wishes, rights, or traditions of others." Relative to our discussion, that definition is right on the mark. If we are to respect diversity, it means we are sensitive to the feelings, rights, and traditions of others. More than this, perhaps, we are curious about them. This is why highly culturally intelligent people are simply more equipped to naturally respect diversity. As already discussed, high-CQ people want to learn more about others and what makes them different from themselves. They remain open to learning more and enjoying more about these differences. They don't see them as threats or negative in any way. On the contrary, they embrace them and leverage them to the benefit of the team, the organization, and the community at large.

Respect means different things to different people, depending on the very things that make each person different, including culture, background, or any other dimension of diversity. Taking the time to find out what respect means to others is a good first step to creating strong relationships that will build personal and professional bridges that will ultimately make people more effective collaborators and able to deliver greater results. Bingo. Isn't that the desired outcome, in any case?

Leaders build cultures and organizations that don't simply celebrate diversity, but they respect it. Here are some questions we can ask to test whether we are respecting diversity in our organizations:

- o How are we making time to learn about cultural differences?
- o Do we have a respectful culture?
- o Where are innovation ideas coming from? Are we using our people's ideas?
- o Are leaders courageous in calling out behaviors?
- o Do we have a culture where people feel heard and valued?
- o Do we allow people to freely voice their opinions?
- o Do we respect and acknowledge special events and holidays of different cultures? Do we respect spirituality and religious beliefs, symbols, and rituals?

Imperative 6. Don't Measure Diversity Numbers; Measure the Results Driven by Diverse Organizations

It seems rather repetitive to continue to quote different data that proves that diverse organizations outperform nondiverse ones. At the risk of stating the obvious again, the facts are that diverse and more inclusive organizations have better employee retention, engagement, and morale. In some surveys I have seen, more than 80 percent of millennials reported higher levels of engagement when they believe their company fosters an inclusive culture. A Boston Consulting Group study found that companies with more diverse management teams have 19 percent higher revenues due to innovation. This is significant for tech companies, start-ups, and industries where innovation is the key to growth. We can quote one study after the next, and we would find that what they all share in common is the fact that diverse organizations outperform nondiverse companies in almost every metric that matters financially.

Despite these facts, companies often focus on measuring a number of diversity-driven metrics. The following are among some of the more common diversity metrics used by companies:

- o *Recruiting and hiring.* As previously discussed, attracting high-caliber talent and creating a strong pipeline of candidates from groups that have been historically underrepresented is critical to a business's long-term sustainability.
- o *Promotions.* The rate of promotions for people of color and underrepresented groups of employees as a percentage of the total employee base is certainly an important metric. Tracking this should help inform talent development and other important strategic decisions.
- o *Retention rates.* No doubt the current trends in attrition are as alarming as they are costly to organizations. Thus, companies need to keep track of the percentage of employees by gender and race, and other dimensions of diversity that may be uniquely relevant to the company, at each level of seniority. They also need to track the movement (e.g., attrition rate) at each of these levels if they are to ensure a strong talent pipeline up and down the ladder.
- o *ERG participation.* When companies have ERGs, there are a number of metrics that typically are put in place, including participation rates, number of members, executive sponsorship, community impact, number of events executed, and amount spent for these events. Unfortunately, that is often the extent of what is measured for the ERGs, and what is lost is the business impact

of having these ERGs in place. ERGs should and can impact important business drivers such as attrition levels, the appeal of the organization as a talent magnet, and industry or community organizational reputation.

o   *Representation.* This may be one of the most important metrics relative to diversity in organizations. It aims directly at what matters most: whether diversity initiatives are simply talk or a truly actionable business imperative within a company. If women, people of color, and employees from other underrepresented groups are not making it to senior levels of the organization, and if there are gaps in representation of these groups in the talent pipeline, it will be obvious to all. The negative impact to attracting, recruiting, and retaining talent will be clearly felt, and the benefit of having a diverse workforce will not be achieved.

There is absolutely nothing wrong with having diversity metrics in place within a company. They are important and necessary. What must also be the case, is that we measure the positive business and financial impact that we enjoy as a result of having a more diverse and inclusive organization. How we measure that will be different from one organization to the next. Leaders must determine the best way to measure the positive impact of diversity on their specific organization. Leaders can ask these questions to test that they are not just focusing on traditional diversity metrics but that they are also getting at the positive business and financial impact of having an inclusive organization:

o   In addition to our typical diversity metrics, how are we measuring the business and financial metrics as a result of having greater diversity in our company?

o   What has been the impact to our talent base in terms of recruiting, retaining, developing, and promoting as a result of having a more diverse organization?

o   How has our innovation pipeline improved over time by having a more inclusive organization? How are ideas generated, vetted, and acted on?

Imperative 7. DE&I Is Not an HR-Driven Activity; It's a Leadership-Driven Imperative

In far too many companies, DE&I is delegated to human resources and is managed as part of the HR function. Even in organizations that have a dedicated chief diversity officer, the activities are primarily managed within the HR team. In fact, when we look at the strategic road maps and their long-range plans, we will almost surely find diversity-related activities, metrics, and financials within HR's strategic plan. More often than not, it is the CHRO who is seen as the champion of diversity in a company. As long as diversity remains a set of activities championed and led primarily by the HR organization, rather than by the CEO and the senior-most leaders of the organization across all functions, it will fail to achieve its full potential and benefit for the company.

This should not be interpreted to mean that HR has no role to play. Clearly, they do. HR can and does support the DE&I process in an organization. Indeed, it may be the best function to administer, track results, and facilitate many of the tactical aspects of how a company supports and maintains an inclusive culture. However, if an organization is truly going to leverage the power of that inclusion, it must be clear that the top leader and the executive teams believe in the power and value of diversity, are fully engaged in the process, and are held accountable for the results and metrics.

Leaders must ensure that the values of diverse and inclusive culture are fully integrated and become part of the key success factors and organizational objectives. There should be no doubt in the direct connection between enabling and supporting an inclusive culture in the company, and the business objectives the organization is striving to achieve. Stated a different way, DE&I needs to be a part of the long-range plan for the company. The strategies, tactics, and budget should be tied directly to the highest levels of the company and championed by the CEO and senior leaders (and the board of directors, if there is one). Moreover, there should be a comprehensive set of metrics (as previously discussed) tied directly to the performance of each of the senior leaders in the company.

One thing is certain: If employees sense a lack of commitment by senior leaders to enable a truly inclusive culture, and they don't see their leaders modeling the right behaviors, they will surely lack the motivation to buy-in. In that case, the power of a diverse and inclusive workforce, even in the event that the company has one in place, will fail to achieve its full potential in terms of results.

It is this diversity imperative, perhaps more than any other, that makes the need for having high-CQ leaders evident. Leaders with high levels of cultural intelligence will be more adept to champion their team in creating a more inclusive culture, consistently modeling the right behaviors, and making an organically diverse thinking mindset the norm at all levels of the organization.

Here are a few questions leaders can ask to ensure that DE&I is not an HR function activity, but a leadership-driven imperative:

o Who is championing diversity in our organization?
o Do we have established CQ and DE&I metrics in place for all leaders and managers?
o Do we have CQ training required for all leaders and managers? How are we incorporating CQ into training at all levels of the organization?

- o How are leaders participating with ERGs?
- o How are leaders demonstrating their belief and support of having a more inclusive culture?

Imperative 8. It's Not about Having a Diverse Workforce, It's about Having Diversity at All Organizational Levels

In our discussion of Imperative 6, we said that one of the important metrics for diversity is that of representation. It's worth expanding on this important idea. Representation in the workforce refers to having employees of different races, religions, ages, genders, ethnicities, and other dimensions of diversity in the mix. However, it has to be more than just having them in the company. For there to be true representation of these different groups, it must be evident across all organizational levels.

It should be obvious that for people to feel more connected to an organization, they would want to see others like them in key leadership and executive roles in the company. Moreover, they would want to see that the pipeline has ample representation of these different backgrounds, as well. This would provide some sense of continuity and a verification that they too could aspire to higher levels within the organization. It would also indicate that the company respects differences and values a more inclusive culture.

The fact still remains that minority groups today continue to be underrepresented, not only in leadership roles but in other higher level roles. According to a study titled "Being Black in Corporate America," blacks fill only 0.8 percent of Fortune 500 CEO roles. Another study from SHRM shows that Asians and Asian Americans make up 8 percent of the board member roles in Fortune 500 companies. Hispanics make up 4 percent of board memberships in Fortune 500 companies. These data only serve as a harsh reminder that despite the talk, perhaps even the good intent, by companies to affect these numbers, progress has been slow. If leaders are to inspire others to follow and to engage for the long term by investing themselves and their talents in the organization, they will do so more willingly if they see themselves represented through the levels of the company.

There is really only one question we need to ask as leaders to ensure that we have a healthy representation and diverse talent pipeline to ensure the sustainability of the enterprise. That question is:

o   Do we have diversity at all levels of the organization, especially the executive teams?

The question is simple. However, if the answer is anything other than a resounding yes, the solution to the problem will not be quite so simple. It will require a concerted effort to change the organizational paradigm and, perhaps, its structure to make room for a more inclusive and diverse team. For a high-CQ leader who understands the value of a diverse organization, this is not an option; it's a business imperative.

Imperative 9. Don't Survey Your Workforce about DE&I; Survey Them about Their Engagement

Employee surveys are one way we can get a sense our employees' mood and concerns. Surveys can help expose issues that impact productivity and engagement. If they are well done, surveys can provide key information that can be leveraged to improve the organizational culture. Surveys need not be complicated. They can range from sophisticated and administered electronically to an old-fashioned suggestion box placed in the company's cafeteria. Conducting employee surveys is generally a good thing. Unfortunately, they often turn into the place where more of the employee complaints and criticisms are voiced, as opposed to where the positive aspects of the company are applauded. Regrettably, these surveys are rarely the source of innovative ideas that drive dramatic change to what we do or how we do it to improve organizational results.

There are many pros to conducting employee surveys:

1. Surveys can provide valuable insights into employee needs and potential ways to improve the organization.
2. They can be a good place for employees to feel free to voice their opinions if they don't otherwise feel comfortable doing so.
3. They can be relatively inexpensive and quick ways to assess the mood of the organization.
4. If the results of surveys are handled well, they can go a long way to creating a more effective culture and even result in lower turnover.

Of course, there are also cons to using employee surveys. Here are a few:

1. Depending on questions asked and the response from management to these surveys, the result can actually be detrimental to the organizational culture. This, of course, is the exact opposite of the desired outcome.
2. It is difficult to know if the answers given during the survey are honest and complete because employees may be suspicious about the process and about their ability to truly remain anonymous.
3. The quality of the questions may not yield answers that can be clearly interpreted or acted on.
4. The response rate may be low, leading to two questions: how valid or representative are the answers to organizational realities, and what to do about the answers given that may not truly represent the majority view?

5. If management does not respond to the surveys, or if nothing is perceived to change after the survey is completed, it could lead to a greater level of disengagement by employees.

There are a few common mistakes that companies make when conducting employee surveys:

1. Conducting surveys either too frequently or not often enough. Fewer than once a year is not sufficient, but doing it monthly or even weekly, as some organizations do, is probably too much. How often we survey is important, and it should be carefully considered given the specific needs of the organization.

2. Asking open-ended questions that generate responses that are vague and difficult to interpret. Moreover, if the questions are poorly phrased, they may be perceived as biased or leading. Leaders should not underestimate the importance of having good scientific methodology to ensure accurate data is driving decision-making. It is best to employ survey experts when engaging in a survey.

3. Not having a robust process for quickly processing data from surveys, debriefing the management team, and formulating actionable plans that can be put in place within a reasonable period of time.

4. Not having clear senior leadership involvement and ownership for the survey results and the actions to be taken in response.

As leadership and management teams weigh these and other pros and cons when deciding whether to conduct employee surveys, they should consider the following: Employee surveys are necessary and valuable if managed appropriately. Importantly, there must be true intent to take action based on the results. Absent this intent, surveys are a waste of time and money. Additionally, it is imperative surveys be done at the appropriate intervals and focus on measuring employee engagement. It is also important to give thoughtful consideration as to what is being asked and why. Finally, there must be a firm plan to take measurable actions with the lessons learned from the information provided in the survey responses.

Imperative 10. Diversity Is Not Exclusive of White; It's Inclusive of All

One of the joys of being a grandfather is putting the baby down to sleep. It's always a special time. When I help put Maddie, my granddaughter, to bed, we always say a prayer, which she likes to extend as long as possible, to keep me laying in the bed next to her for a little longer. I know one day, I will long for those times when she was a little girl, so I enjoy every bit of them now.

As I was saying goodnight to her tonight, April 17, 2022, I asked her this question: "Maddie, I need your help with something. Can you help me remember the name of all the colors?"

She didn't hesitate for a moment and went right into her answer. She said, "Let's see …" (Yes, at five and half years old, she started her sentence with "Let's see."). "Let's see, there is red, blue, my favorite pink, purple, orange, black, gray, white, yellow, and ummm, oh, I know, brown." She went on to explain how she likes pink the most.

I then asked her, "So white is a color too?"

Her response was a simple "Of course." Then after she thought about it a bit more, she added, "It's not the prettiest color, but of course it's a color."

I nodded at her in approval and said, "Thank you, Maddie, that helped me a lot."

After further pondering, she said, "But wait, bunnies are white, right? And everyone likes bunnies, so white is a nice color too."

I laughed out loud. I guess she wanted to make sure we had not hurt white's feelings. From the mouth of a five-year-old child comes the wisdom that white is a color too.

The term "people of color," which has come to be synonymous with diversity, has been rather exclusively reserved for every other color except white; it specifically excludes white men. It seems ironic that the very effort to create inclusive cultures in organizations via diversity programs and initiatives excludes one of the most important stakeholders in the process. If we are to list reasons why diversity programs have failed to significantly, sustainably, and permanently move the needle over the past several decades, we would have to start the list by listing "excluding white males" as one of the top reasons.

In her *Harvard Business Review* article "How to Show White Men That Diversity and Inclusion Efforts Need Them,"[15] published in October 2019, Lily Zheng wrote this:

> Some white male leaders don't feel like they have a role to play in diversity and inclusion efforts, or that they don't belong in discussions about how to help less privileged people in their organizations. If you want the support of people with privilege—making them allies, rather than enemies—it's important to offer psychologically safe spaces for white people and privileged people to explore their identities and concerns. Otherwise, you will continue to encounter defensiveness and a lack of full support.

I am tempted to end this section in the chapter with a simple "Are there any questions?" Zheng's remarks hit the nail on the head. The simple reality is that without everyone's involvement in the workplace, diversity initiatives will fail. We don't want everyone to feel like they belong except the white men. We need everyone to feel they belong. We need everyone to understand they play an important role in creating and living the culture we work in.

We could have a healthy - and lengthy - debate to discuss all the reasons why white men have been excluded from the DE&I process. At a minimum, whether purposefully or simply by neglect, we can likely all agree that they have not been included much other than to be often accused of being the root of most of the problems. I suppose that seems reasonable, given that historically, and still today, they've held the power and privilege position. However, we can also likely agree that in many cases, they have been demonized much to the detriment of the diversity process, if creating an inclusive, collaborative culture was the end game. Whatever past reasons we had for excluding them, what is important is a realization that white is a color too, and white men need to be part of the diversity process as much as anyone else. This is why I believe so fundamentally that the solution in the long term begins with making everyone culturally intelligent. The high-CQ person understands that it's not about color, religion, or any other dimension of diversity you care to list. Rather, it's about understanding where we come from, how we show up, how others are, and how they show up, and finding the best way to communicate and work across these differences.

If we are going to bring white men into the mix, we should probably start with understanding why more of them are not engaged in the DE&I process. Here too the reasons can be many and varied. No doubt some may simply not get it or care since they have not felt impacted by any form of discrimination or sense of not belonging. Others may be openly angry or hostile towards the process as they may see it as a threat to their own advancement, feeling they have been maligned for nothing they have done directly themselves. I can understand that. Imagine if you were told "you're the problem" when you may not even understand what they problem is, or worse than this, you don't feel you have done anything to create the problem. It should not be too difficult for us to empathize with their feelings. This may be a good place to start if we are to encourage them to be a part of the longer term solution.

Some white men may not be willing to engage in the process. However, I believe given the chance and being encouraged to do so in the right ways, many men, white or any other color, will be motivated to be a part of the process, even if they are unsure of how to do it. That's the second thing we must do if we are to include the white men: help them to become involved and encourage them in constructive ways. We can start by making sure the current diversity initiatives that are in place in the company do not put white men on the defensive. We should create a safe environment for the learning that comes along with becoming culturally intelligent and learning to deal with unconscious bias. The bottom line is that we all have stuff to work on, not just the white guy.

Consider the enduring positive impact that would be felt if the men currently in power were brought on board and became involved and true champions of diversity initiatives. This would be a perfect combination of grassroots movements meeting leadership imperatives, with the bottom and the top coming together like never before. For this to happen, men who feel excluded need to understand how they will benefit from more diverse cultures and how they can become champions of a better way of working.

Here are some simple questions we can ask to test if we are engaging everyone, including white men, in the company's DE&I process:

- o What are we doing proactively to involve everyone in the DE&I process?
- o How are we engaging with the white men in the organization?
- o Are ERGs evolving into inclusive BRGs?
- o How are we fostering a culture of true inclusivity?

The aim of this chapter was to challenge all of us to reconsider our DE&I strategies and encourage leaders to break the old paradigms. The world has changed and continues to change at an alarmingly fast pace. The DE&I process that may have worked in your company ten or twenty years ago are outdated and ineffective. Moreover, there is no one-size-fit-all DE&I strategy that works for all organizations. There are some principles that can be adapted to help create cultures that support DE&I processes and help organizations gain from the benefits of being organically diversity minded teams. The key to this lies in the organization's ability to be continuously learning and adaptable, building a strong foundation with cultural intelligence at all levels of the organization, and ensuring that the top ten DE&I imperatives inform what we do and how we measure it.

A few final thoughts on driving effective DE&I strategies. First, we have to come to terms with the fact that there will be resistance to change. It's a common outcome with the implementation of DE&I programs that there will be some employees who will resist it, some outwardly and others in a passive-aggressive way. We should deal with this resistance the same way we do with resistance to any other important company initiative:

1. Try to understand the causes of the resistance and do your best to address the concerns raised.
2. Be crystal clear on the strategic imperative and the rationale for treating it as a business priority.
3. Reaffirm leadership's commitment and expectations.

4. Provide those resisting the change an opportunity to participate and come onboard with the initiative.

5. After providing feedback and trying to ensure that those resisting the change are heard, included, and involved, if their resistance continues, perhaps they don't fit in the organization and should be assisted in exiting the team. That may seem a bit extreme, but over the years, I have learned the hard way that allowing dissent among the ranks for too long is corrosive and detrimental to the organization. It is best to deal with the dissenters directly and swiftly.

Second, a poorly executed DE&I strategy may be worse than not doing anything. Initiatives that have as their foundation old-fashioned ideas and ineffective trainings will only add to the diversity fatigue that so many people already feel. Leaders should make sure they work as hard on developing the correct DE&I strategy as they do any other business imperative. Engage experts when necessary, and establish the correct metrics based on what we discussed in this chapter. Finally, leaders must realize that for DE&I initiatives to take hold in their organizations, and if they are to build lasting cultures that are organically diverse thinking ones, they have to remain consistent and persistent in their support and leadership on DE&I.

In the reality of our global economy, leaders must create these respectful and inclusive environments that leverage all dimensions of diversity if they ever hope to be truly competitive. Having leaders and entire teams in the organization who are able to seamlessly move between cultures, understand different points of view, be open to consider different ways to operate, and enjoy being collaborative is a sure way to ensure success. High-CQ leaders and teams will better leverage diversity and inclusion, and in a world that will never stop being diverse, this is a significant advantage.

PART 4

The Board's and Executive Team's
Role in Culture and Enabling CQ

CHAPTER 10

The Four Dimensions of Board Oversight

Most leaders agree on the importance of corporate culture. The best leaders focus on it as a business imperative and driver. They understand that culture is defined by a set of accepted behaviors, beliefs, and values common to all in the organization. Great leaders depend on the culture to influence levels of engagement and trust in discussions and decisions made up and down the organization. Importantly, great leaders know that while the culture of an organization is a shared responsibility by all members of the team, it is the senior most executive leaders and the board of directors who play a key and active role in the process of creating the right culture.

Although boards are typically removed from the day-to-day operations and management decisions, they still play a critically important part in modeling the correct values. It is clear that the individual performance and behaviors for each board member, as well as their actions as a collective group, set a tone from the top that sends loud and clear signals to all levels of the organization. Moreover, in their primary capacity to hold the CEO accountable and providing oversight of the business, they must understand the importance of culture on the overall team's performance. Not all companies, however, have a board of directors, although they have a leader and leadership teams. Thus, in this chapter, as we explore the actions that those at the top must take to drive organizational culture effectively, we interchangeably refer to the board of directors (BOD) and the executive leadership team (ELT).

ELTs have many functions, including creating strategies and tactical plans, outlining a growth road map and associated financial projections, building the best teams from the top to the bottom of the organization, and assessing opportunities and risk. In most cases, the better companies and teams have well-established processes for managing their business planning cycles and measuring their successes and failures. They certainly have well-defined risk management processes, and in companies with BODs, committees are established to ensure business focus areas are assessed properly. Hence the existence of the governance, audit, and risks committees.

However, one area that is not always so well represented in terms of oversight of ELT focus is organizational culture. This is changing quickly, with many companies trying to figure out how to manage culture as they do other business drivers: with objectives, metrics, and leadership accountability.

With this newfound recognition of the importance of culture, the question becomes: how should leaders go about establishing and fostering the desired culture? And what is the best way to measure their progress along the way? For the companies with a board, what role can they play while making sure not to interfere with the CEO and management team in their responsibilities of running the operation? the NACD Blue Ribbon Commission on Culture drew the following important conclusion:

> Directors and company leaders should take a forward-
> looking, proactive approach to culture oversight in order

to achieve a level of discipline that is comparable to leading practices in the management and oversight of risk.

To effectively do that, there are four dimensions of cultural oversight that boards and leadership teams must consider and make an integral part of their workflow: board culture, CEO and executive team CQ, organizational culture, and organizational and brand reputation. These are briefly described in figure 4. Next, let's unpack each of these in detail.

Figure 4: Board of Directors and Executive Team's
Four Dimensions of Cultural Oversight

Dimension 1: Board Culture

Establishing the Importance and Value of Corporate Culture

The COVID pandemic that began in 2020 fundamentally altered the way companies operate. Certainly through 2020 and into 2021, as companies struggled to figure out how to conduct their businesses with a remote workforce, it became increasingly apparent to many what the true state and condition of their organizational culture is. It was a test for many companies as to whether their values and expected norms and behaviors would hold or be effective in a new, nontraditional management structure. Suddenly, the old-fashioned management hierarchy was exposed as just that: old-fashioned. Useless, in fact. Managers had to learn to trust their employees to work remotely, away from daily oversight and the structure of the office environment. Suddenly, employees had to figure out how to do their jobs primarily from home while avoiding the obvious distractions that come along with that.

How companies dealt with the pandemic, the safety of their employees and customers, and the emphasis they placed on trying to run their business to protect the top and bottom line was exposed for all to see. Compound these overwhelmingly difficult circumstances with the civil unrest we witnessed in many cities, movements such as Black Lives Matter, the calls for defunding the police, and what we experienced was a perfect storm. Some businesses did very well, as the pandemic caused a boom in their products and services, while others struggled to keep the doors open. One thing is certain, though: All companies were transformed in some way. That means the pre-COVID organizational culture is not the same as what has evolved in the post-COVID era. Thus, the first thing a board and leadership team have to establish and agree on is this: Corporate culture is important, and we must deal with it as a business imperative. It cannot be left to evolve on its own at the whims of environmental factors.

In his June 4, 2019, article "The Board's Role in Corporate Culture,"[16] published in *Diligent Insights*, Rick Hoel wrote this:

> A healthy corporate culture is a valuable asset, a source of competitive advantage and vital to the creation and protection of long-term value. It is the board's role to determine the purpose of the company and to ensure that the company's values, strategy and business model are aligned to its purpose. Directors should not wait for a crisis before they focus on company culture. In addition, the Board should be continually inquisitive about other

successful companies that are developing unique cultural paradigms.

He is absolutely correct.

Setting the Tone from the Top

A culture is effective only if it is lived and modeled by those at the top. The board and CEO have the responsibility to consistently exhibit the behaviors that bring the stated values to life. Everything they do, and everything they say, sets the tone. There is no clearer evidence of this than thinking about the significant impact that occurs when the leader of an organization becomes embroiled in some scandal, whether internal or external to the organization, and how this affects every aspect of the company.

In today's world of videos gone viral, reputational risks are often considered as great as strategic, operating, or financial risks. We have all seen the damaging impacts of one social media post and the harm done in an instant to individuals and companies. Never before in history has there been such exposure and transparency of information, even if it's not intended. Information always gets out. Every cell phone is a potential source of a leak. Pictures, texts, and videos travel across the globe in mere seconds, and there is no putting the genie back in the bottle.

Here's what Nicole Standford, a partner and regulatory and operational risk market leader for Deloitte Risk and Financial Advisory, Deloitte & Touche LLP, wrote this in a 2018 *Wall Street Journal* article.[17]

> The tone at the top sets an organization's guiding values and ethical climate. Properly fed and nurtured, it is the

foundation upon which the culture of an enterprise is built.

What should leaders do to establish the right tone at the top? They need to start by recognizing that this requires a continuous effort and a very clear alignment by all members of the board and executive team. The expected norms and behavior standards that support the organizational values must not just be words written on the wall or the company's website. They should be discussed frequently and purposefully to make them innate and a part of the team's modus operandi. In the same article mentioned above, Standford quoted Keith Darcy, an independent senior advisor to Deloitte & Touche LLP, who stated:

> Creating and maintaining the right tone at the top is the bedrock of a robust ethics and compliance program. By clarifying and then carefully harmonizing the relevant roles of the CEO, board and CCO, organizations can establish a tone at the top that truly binds the organization together.

Embedding Culture as an Auditable Imperative

Earlier in the book, we defined corporate culture. We described it as the unwritten rules that set expectations for how people behave. It is reflected by what people actually do. You can see it by what is rewarded and celebrated. You can also see it in what behaviors are tolerated or even overlooked in some cases. Here's the most important thing about culture: It is how companies create value through people. Since value can and should be measured, it's imperative that boards determine the most effective way that they should embed culture as an auditable imperative.

In their May 2019 article "Five Ways to Enhance Board Oversight of Culture,"[18] published by EY, Joe Dettmann and Stephen Klemash wrote this:

> A company's intangible assets, which include talent and culture, are now estimated to make up 52% of a company's market value. And for some companies, it can be as high as 90%. This is higher than at any point in modern history, and most likely to accelerate. Today, company value is defined less by industrial-era physical assets like plants and equipment and more by information-age human capital. It is clearer than ever that a company's talent, and the culture that enables that talent, are sources of quantifiable competitive differentiation.
>
> For these reasons, oversight of culture is a growing priority in the boardroom—and rightly so. The board plays a critical oversight role for various dimensions that shape culture. Responsibility for defining the right culture for the company and embedding it within daily operations falls to management, but the board must oversee and hold management to account on how it is defining, aligning (to purpose and strategy), embodying and reporting on culture.

There is no doubt there is increasing pressure from shareholders, investors, and even some regulatory bodies to hold boards and leadership teams accountable for creating and maintaining effective cultures as one important driver of sustained business results.

There are several steps boards or leadership teams can take to support management in establishing and leveraging culture:

1. Bring the voice of culture to the boardroom
2. Champion cultural intelligence and the DE&I process in the company
   a. Evaluate the board's culture and CQ index
3. Measure how culture is communicated, modeled, and lived by leaders
4. Ensure rewards and recognitions are aligned with organizational culture objectives

Let's discuss these further.

Bring the Voice of Culture to the Boardroom

The first step to making culture an auditable imperative is making sure it is a part of the agenda. Like any other business imperative, organizational culture needs to be included in the normal process for the board. The old adage of "What gets measured gets done" most certainly applies here. In some cases, boards and ELTs have established independent committees with the assigned charter for cultural oversight. In other cases, special committees have been put in place to ensure the process and metrics are established, and that some group within the leadership team is held accountable for making sure it remains an actionable item on the board's agenda. In most cases, cultural oversight will likely be well placed within the governance committee of a board, with strong links to the compensation committee to ensure that the most important driver of success as it relates to cultural oversight actually happens. That is this: Ensure there is a link and alignment between culture and the company's vision and strategy, and the way executives are measured and rewarded.

Good culture won't develop by writing memos and posting them in the company newsletter. Often, certain functions and departments within the organization are seen as the champions of the process, such as HR, Compliance, Audit, or even Legal. However, everyone in the organization needs to know and live the culture. The board's role here is critical in three ways: First, the board should bring representatives of these groups to report on organizational culture metrics and employee surveys related to culture. This will keep the board's finger on organizational health. Second, the board should look for ways to understand the reputational health of the organization from external sources. Finally, boards should ensure that teams are empowered and resourced to be able to deliver on the strategic objectives related to organizational culture.

Champion Cultural Intelligence and the DE&I Process in the Company

Building on the previous point on how boards can bring the voice of culture into the boardroom, they can and must go beyond that to actually champion the process. Here are some actionable ways this can be accomplished:

1. Consider creating a culture oversight committee to manage similarly as others such as audit, governance, and HR. This will bring structure and accountability to this important area and make it a part of the board's oversight strategy.
2. Establish a process (at least annually or semiannually) for evaluating and offering guidance to the company's DE&I strategy, as presented by the CEO and chief diversity officer or other key leaders.
3. Invite ERG leaders to participate in listening sessions, where they can present their strategies and accomplishments as a way of providing visibility at the board level.

4. Establish board-level champions and sponsors for key ERGs. This should be done in partnership with members of the executive team, who should have an active sponsorship role for ERGs. As always, board members have to be thoughtful about maintaining their independence and management distance, and deciding if they are to play a role as ERG sponsors. This should indeed be limited to offering support and advice but not being involved in the strategic direction established by the leadership team, as it relates to diversity initiatives in the company.

5. The board can encourage all members to complete a CQ assessment. Then in a facilitated discussion, board members can share their assessments and discuss their personal plans to improve their CQ index. The board can also have a board-level assessment done of their collective CQ and then discuss specific actions they can take to improve the team's overall cultural intelligence index.

6. Consider engaging an external expert to assess the overall board culture and effectiveness. Evaluating the overall organizational DE&I strategy, objectives, and metrics should be completed annually.

Measure How Culture Is Communicated, Modeled, and Lived by Leaders

Culture and leadership are inextricably linked. The values influential leaders often set in motion become imprinted in the organization and can persist long after they are gone. Over time, an organization's leaders shape culture, through both conscious and unconscious actions. The very best leaders are fully aware of their role in culture. They own it, think about it, and act in ways consistent to the culture they want to have evolve within their teams. Some leaders, unfortunately, delegate or abdicate their responsibility to HR and treat culture not as a business imperative, but as something we talk about once in a while.

Like culture itself, leadership as it relates to organizational culture can be challenging to measure. Beyond the financial and diversity metrics that have become somewhat standard in companies, trying to measure less-tangible objectives can be difficult and somewhat subjective. Pulse surveys can be a great way of gaining feedback from employees, and questions can center around how the workforce regards leaders within the organization. In addition to these sorts of instruments, boards and executive leadership teams can also do the following:

1. Consider the leader's behaviors.
    b. For instance, how often do leaders speak about culture, and do they behave in ways consistent to that cultural expectation?
    c. Has the leader insisted on having a detailed, thoughtful plan for strategy and execution relative to organizational culture?
2. Ensure that leaders have specific organizational culture and DE&I metrics that they are held accountable for.
3. Insist that leaders learn about and are measured against their Cultural Intelligence Index. Over the past three decades, a leader's Emotional Intelligence Index has become a normal and well-accepted metric to measure effectiveness. Moreover, leaders are often coached and educated on how to improve their EQ. The leader's cultural intelligence should be managed similarly. There are many tools available to measure a leader's CQ index, and as previously discussed in this book, CQ can be coached and developed. Boards should insist that leaders in the organization take that CQ journey seriously.

4. Board can expect leaders to demonstrate a desire to develop and evolve in their cultural intelligence.

Ensure Rewards and Recognitions Are Aligned with Organizational Culture Objectives

There is only one saying that overrides "What gets measured gets done," and that is "What gets rewarded becomes priority." All the evidence we need to know this is true can be found if we look at our behavior relative to how we are compensated or otherwise rewarded. We may say we want people in our organization to behave a particular way, but if the way we recognized them says something else, we should not be surprised at which kind of behavior we will actually get from them.

The reward system we put in place will communicate the behavioral norms culture to all members of the team, new and old, and affirm the true culture of the organization. The reward system thus functions as a primary instrument for acculturation and control by transmitting values and norms throughout the company.

Therefore, the reward system should support and encourage those behaviors that are consistent with all the company stands for. Moreover, this reward system should be monitored and reviewed at least annually to ensure that it is evolved as necessary to support the cultural development of the organization. The board's role here is clear: ensure there is strict alignment between the company's vision, strategy, stated values, and expected behavioral norms, and the way people are rewarded and compensated.

Dimension 2. CEO and Executive Team CQ

Just as before, It Starts with the Tone at the Top

The second dimension of board cultural oversight has to do with the cultural intelligence of the CEO and the members of the executive team. As we have already established, organizations led by high-CQ leaders are better performing companies. That is why boards should concern themselves with ensuring that those at the top of the organization are constantly growing as high-CQ leaders.

The starting point for setting the tone begins with the organization's governing authority; generally, this means the board of directors. The board's most fundamental tasks typically include hiring the CEO, approving strategy, monitoring execution of the plan, setting risk appetite, and exercising appropriate oversight regarding risk mitigations, with the goal of preserving and creating shareholder value. But of all the board's responsibilities, chief among them is hiring and managing (and, when necessary, firing) the CEO. There is a very important reason why this is the board's primary responsibility: The tone at the top is established by the CEO and by extension her leadership team. It's not surprising, therefore, that boards focus on competence, character, and chemistry when selecting their CEOs. They weigh many traits and characteristics, track record of results, emotional intelligence, and other important criteria when making their selection. There is no doubt in my mind that cultural intelligence must become an additional selection criterion for CEOs and key executives in any company.

To have the right tone at the top, leaders must be able to effectively connect with people inside and outside the organization. After all, CEOs are the face of the organization. They are who employees ultimately look to for vision, guidance, and leadership. It's the CEO, and the entire leadership team, people will emulate most in terms of daily behaviors.

Another important factor in leaders being able to establish the right tone at the top is their perceived credibility. Leaders who consistently communicate and walk their values enjoy higher levels of credibility than those who don't. It's that simple. It is also simple to understand why leaders with high CQ are more effective in demonstrating these credibility-building behaviors more fluidly that those with lower levels of CQ (or none at all).

The bottom line is this: The leader who sets the right tone at the top will ensure a healthy mood in the middle and an empowered feeling throughout the organization. The only possible result of this is a high-performing winning organization.

Benchmarking and Developing High-CQ Leaders

In recent years, one of the most important developments in the field of cultural intelligence has been the emergence of a number of assessment tools and inventories that measure intercultural competence. As we have already discussed, these cultural intelligence assessments can provide individuals and organizations with valuable insights into the areas they need to pay attention to in terms of their development. These tools have been developed using verified scientific methodologies and can provide information that enables individuals to turn abstract ideas about what CQ is and how they compare to others on a number of CQ index scales, into a measurable and actionable CQ improvement plan.

In addition, there are intercultural assessment tools that can be used to gauge how culturally intelligent organizations are, providing a good foundation from which to evolve. Importantly, these same tools can be used as part of the recruiting and onboarding process to help new team members succeed in culturally diverse environments.

There are many intercultural assessments available with different constructs and ways of measuring individual and organizational competence in this area. Thus, selecting the right one for your company can be a challenge. It's important that leaders give careful consideration to what the end in mind is in doing these sorts of assessments. Some intercultural inventories assess an individual's traits and demographic characteristics; these are areas that typically do not change and are not responsive to interventions. As is the case with other personality and leadership style inventories, such as Myers-Briggs, these sorts of inventories provide good insights into individual competence as it relates to cultural intelligence but may not be much help in determining how to develop it. There are other inventories that focus on assessing attitudes and beliefs that develop in early childhood through unconscious socialization. These are what we refer to our implicit biases or unconscious biases, and they too will be difficult to change, although being aware of them is critical to being able to learn to manage them, even if we can't change them.

Other inventories focus on measuring the skills one possesses to be effective in an intercultural context. These are the ones that in this author's opinion begin to get to the point of CQ assessments: help individuals understand their individual competencies relative to the traits of high-CQ individuals, and clearly identify the specific areas that can be developed and enhanced by training, goal setting, and direct involvement in intercultural activities and interactions. These action-oriented instruments assess our desire, intent, knowledge, and capability to improve how we interact across differences.

Thus, again, when selecting an assessment instrument, it is very important to be clear on what it is we are trying to measure and what we want the end outcome to be. Start by consulting an expert in this area who can assist with making a determination on the best tool available for your leaders and your particular organization. From the research I have done, and from personal experience, I believe one of the best sources of information, cultural intelligence assessments, and even some consulting and training services, is the Cultural Intelligence Center. Based in Grand Rapids, Michigan, and founded by Dr. David Livermore, the company is a research-based training and consulting firm that helps organizations and individuals assess and improve their CQ. As it relates to testing instruments, they have a number of excellent on-line assessments that are straightforward, are easy to administer, and provide a terrific report out on the individual that essentially creates a road map for personal improvement.

The Cultural Intelligence Center offers a variety of excellent tools that can be applied, depending on whether you are trying to measure individual capabilities or personal preferences. They also have assessments that measure Cultural Intelligence (CQ) and Cultural Values (CV). The difference between these is significant. The CQ Assessments measure an individual's capability to work and relate effectively with people from different nationalities, ethnicities, and cultural backgrounds; the Cultural Values profile measures individual preferences that influence approaches to life, school, and work. In my view, it's the two together that provide the most complete picture and action plan for improvement.

The bottom line on benchmarking and developing the leader's CQ is that the board and executive leadership team retain the key responsibility for driving a high-powered culture. One very important step in creating this culture is helping develop high-CQ leaders because the data are clear that high-CQ leaders create high-CQ organizations, and high-CQ organizations generate better results than those with lower CQ.

Dimension 3. Organizational Culture

Throughout this book, we have established the importance of organizational culture and the key role leaders and, by extension, boards play in driving it. The third dimension of oversight has to do with how we measure and check that organizational culture is not lost as a business imperative. There are four specific ways that boards and leadership teams can do that.

1. Living the values. Boards and leadership teams must ask themselves this very important question: Are we living our values? Are our leaders truly embodying and modeling the behaviors expected in order to support the stated organizational values? It's a simple but profound question. Any answer other than a resounding yes requires that we explore any gaps and agree on specific actions that will be taken to close them.

2. Talent development. Most companies have a talent development process. Too often, however, it is seen as a once-a-year exercise that managers have to do in order to meet some mandated deadline to check an HR box. If that sounds harsh, perhaps it is, but in more than thirty years, I have experienced this cycle of talent development quite a number of times across many companies. Where I have seen it work best is when leaders made it a clear mandate to drive this process. The talent development process is how we can understand the talent pool and pipeline we have in our organization to ensure our competitive advantage. It is also the one way we can identify the talent gaps that prevent us from achieving greatness. Thus, the board and the executive leadership team need to ensure we have a robust, actionable, and consistent talent development process in place.

3. Engagement and belonging. When it comes to organizational culture, these two words (engagement and belonging) encapsulate the essence of what leaders need their people to feel when they

are part of the team. As we discussed in chapter 9, creating a culture where people feel they are challenged, and all their skills are leveraged leads to them feeling engaged with the organization. Indeed, it makes them feel like they belong; they are respected, acknowledged, and valued. When people feel they belong, they deliver their very best to the team. Clearly, the board and the ELT need to measure the level of engagement and belonging their team members feel. This is a key indicator of culture and a huge driver of retention.

4. Top ten DE&I imperatives. In the previous chapter, we covered these ten imperatives. We discussed the ways boards and leadership teams must ensure they are focusing on the right aspects of culture and DE&I strategy, with the appropriate metrics that truly reflect the desired organizational outcomes. As part of their overall oversight, and in order to have a complete picture of organizational culture, the board and the leadership team should continuously ask probing questions that challenge the status quo and test for real progress in these areas of DE&I.

Dimension 4. Company and Brand Reputation

Good leaders understand the importance of their companies' reputations. A company with strong positive reputations attracts better people, retain clients longer, and over time do better financially. A company with a great reputation is perceived as providing more value and that in turn allows them to position themselves as a premium brand in the marketplace. They enjoy customer loyalty and shareholder trust. A good brand reputation enables a company to be perceived as uniquely positioned, credible, and desirable by customers. We all feel good when we purchase that brand. This intangible asset, a brand's good reputation, is the most valuable in a company's inventory, and it must be protected.

In his December 2019 article "The Importance of Brand Reputation: 20 Years to Build, Five Minutes to Ruin,"[19] published in *Forbes* magazine, Paul Blanchard wrote:

> The ICCO recently published its World PR Report 2020, detailing the views of public relations companies for the forthcoming year. It's a weighty document, well researched and authoritative. To give a sense of the scale, it draws on responses from 3,000 agency heads operating in the ICCO's 41 member associations. For me, the standout finding was that reputation, the core mission of my business, is consistently ranked by corporate leaders as their most valuable asset. More than that, it is expected to be a key area of growth over the next five years.

Blanchard explains that the "appetite" for reputation management and advice is driven by two impulses: first, proactively seeking to project a positive image of a person, brand, or enterprise. Second, reactively fearing a sudden crisis or media disaster that will rock the company boat severely. The key point is the two impulses he points out: proactive and reactive. Many companies don't give this sufficient emphasis in a proactive way, but rather it takes some event, usually negative, for them to take note and respond.

Boards and ELTs must protect the reputation of the company and their brand. As part of their cultural oversight, they must have a clear view of what that reputation is and how it is evolving. They must also understand this from several perspectives:

1. The internal view: How do our employees perceive our company and brand reputation?

2. The external view: How do shareholders, investors, customers, and partners view our reputation?

3. The candidate view: This is how potential employees view our company and our brands. It goes directly to our ability to be a talent magnet and attract the very best talent to our organization.

There are a number of good tools available for boards and executive leadership teams to assess a company's reputation and brand reputation. As part of their oversight responsibilities, they should avail themselves of the right tool to ensure they are capturing, analyzing, and interpreting data on the company's reputation. Managing the risks associated with brand and company reputation should receive as much attention, if not more, as do financial, cybersecurity, environmental, competitive, and other risks.

The board should see itself as the guardian of the organization's reputation. They should ensure that reputation management is embedded within the board's oversight and a part of the overall enterprise risk management. While neither the board nor the ELT can completely eliminate reputational risks, they can take steps to prepare for them and have solid plans in place to mitigate them. Boards should hold CEOs and their teams accountable for having a robust process for monitoring and assessing the company's reputation and reporting back on the appropriate actions being taken proactively to deal with these risks.

The quality of data that can be acquired to provide insights from the different key stakeholders (internal and external) on the corporate reputation will determine the quality of the mitigation plans. The old adage "garbage in, garbage out" certainly applies here. It is imperative that companies gain valuable and actionable insights from shareholders, employees, the general public, government and regulatory bodies, and any other important constituent if they are going to really understand the company's and brand's reputation. The fact is that the risks to reputation have become increasingly sophisticated and technology enabled. Everything from accidental open-microphone faux pas with leaders being caught making inappropriate remarks, to cell phone videos exposing some less-than-desirable action by anyone in the organization, the company reputation is fragile and under constant threat.

Thus, the tools we use to gain useful insights should be equally as sophisticated and nimble. One such tool was created by CulturIntel, a company founded just a few short years ago by Enrique Arbelaez and Lili Gil Valletta, and where I am privilege to serve as an advisor. Using the power of artificial intelligence, CulturIntel analyzes every available open-source digital discussion to discover patterns in public sentiment, understand people's needs, and deliver actionable insights that represent the unsolicited voice of the people.

CulturIntel goes beyond just social listening. Whereas many tools can do what is referred to as buzz tracking (measuring the amount of noise) and social media listening (monitoring what people are saying without understanding the social or cultural context), this sophisticated tool is culturally intelligent and provides deep insights, taking into account the intent and cultural context of the conversation, to not only understand what they are saying but why they are saying it. This enables an understanding of the cultural, behavioral, and contextual dynamics that impact people's decisions. Moreover, CulturIntel may be the only currently available tech solution that trains the AI tool with inclusion in mind. That means the tool looks at the data through the lens of gender, ethnicity, geography, and cultural context to deliver personalized and actionable insights.

Perhaps another way to think about this methodology is not as a replacement of traditional research, but as a way to flip the method upside down. Research today is designed for validation; typically, with a pre-set list of questions to validate a hypothesis or confirm assumptions about the people or issues that are being targeted in the assessment. Rather than designing a questionnaire or leading the discussion, the CulturIntel algorithm discovers patterns in topics, unmet needs, and sentiment drivers from all available real-time, unsolicited, and authentic digital discussion. It's basically a quantitative analysis of the qualitative data produced by the digital voice of the people.

Whatever tools boards and executive leadership teams choose to use, the point is simple: They must have a credible, repeatable, and effective way to monitor the company's and brand's reputation. They must ensure that as part of the culture oversight process, there are actionable strategies and plans being put into play each day to protect this most valuable asset: the company's reputation

Boards are recognizing that a healthy board culture is an important element of board performance. Unlike other areas of board governance, board culture is probably less clearly defined and understood. It is highly likely that if you ask board members to describe the culture of their team, they will use general terms. Words such as "collaborative" and "highly competent" are commonly used to describe the culture of the board. No doubt that is true of most boards and executive teams. However, boards have to go deeper to truly gain an understanding of their culture and how they operate as a team. What about their diversity of thought? Do they collectively view global business issues through a broader lens, and do they incorporate cultural dynamics in their discussions? Getting down to the individual CQ of each board member, as well as their collective cultural intelligence, and having honest, fact-based discussions on the culture of the board is no longer optional if a board wants to operate at peak levels of effectiveness.

Moreover, while boards many not be in a position to carry out the strategies necessary to create a desired culture in the organization, they surely can be responsible for their own culture as a team and what they model as a leadership group. Most certainly, they are responsible for holding the CEO and other key leaders in the organization accountable for driving the culture and all its dimensions to the benefit of the company. Importantly, with the recent increase in scrutiny on board performance and the movement to have diverse boards, the topic of board culture, and their role in organizational cultural oversight, has become ever more relevant and urgent. Therefore, the only reasonable conclusion is that boards must make board culture and board oversight of organizational culture a part of their fiduciary responsibilities and create a governance guidance to include it as a part of their annual board agenda.

CONCLUSION

Those who are privileged to lead bear an awesome burden. Leaders, CEOs, executive leadership team members, board members, and other individuals in a position of influence (formal or otherwise) have an awesome responsibility to be their very best. It is only then that those they lead can be nurtured, developed, challenged, and unleashed to accomplish their greatness. We need, in fact, we expect, intelligent leaders who have healthy levels of emotional intelligence and an abundance of cultural intelligence.

Cultural intelligence is a must-have trait of a strong, effective leader. Today's global environment demands it. High-CQ leaders can adapt to multicultural situations and use their understanding of the diversity within their team to build strategies that drive breakthrough results. Reaching a high degree of CQ as a leader starts with developing strong cultural proprioception, and that is accomplished by

o   becoming increasingly self-aware,
o   always adapting and learning from our experiences,
o   seeking proactively to understand others and their cultures,
o   understanding our own biases, triggers, and response mechanisms,
o   developing a healthy habit of seeking feedback to drive behavioral modifications, and
o   remaining culturally curious and being a lifelong learner.

Leaders who recognize the importance of cultural intelligence invest in their own development and that of their team. Often, this can be aided by conducting workshops and training on CQ and incorporating a model such as the one presented here, to guide an organization in incorporating CQ into their daily routine. The power of cultural intelligence is unleashed when all members of the organization, especially those privileged to lead, embrace their own journey of developing CQ, achieve a high level of cultural proprioception, model the right behaviors, and become infusion accelerators. They will be rewarded with high-performing, breakthrough-thinking teams that create cultures that attract and retain the very best talent and achieve sustained results, and that's a great legacy for a leader to aspire to.

The journey to becoming a high-CQ person is lifelong. We will always be able to learn and adapt our thinking and behaviors as we gain experience and broaden our horizons through every interaction in our personal and professional lives. If we remain open to growth and change, and if we learn to suspend judgment, then our transformation will flourish. Armed with increasing levels of inward and outward cultural proprioception, we will become great models of the right behaviors. If we are willing to do the work of understanding the strength of the diversity each individual brings to build strategies that resonate across the broader organization, then we will become powerful infusion accelerators. Leaders who reap the reward of building high-CQ organizations think and behave in organically diverse ways and inevitably deliver better long-term results.

I hope you have found this book helpful. I trust it will motivate you to explore your cultural intelligence and embark on the journey to transform yourself into a better human being. High-CQ leaders are better leaders. They know they need to create a high-CQ organization so they can influence thinking from the boardroom to the mailroom.

One final thought on becoming a high-CQ leader: High-CQ leaders create legacies that outlast them. High-CQ leaders will be remembered long after they are gone and leave a legacy that those who love them most can be proud of. I can only hope that I will be able to accomplish that in my lifetime. God bless you, and enjoy your journey.

REFERENCES

1. "Culture as a Corporate Asset," 2007 Blue-Ribbon Commission report, National Association of Corporate Directors (NACD).

2. *Frames of Mind: The Theory of Multiple Intelligences*, 1983, Howard Gardner.

3. *Emotional Intelligence*, 1996, Dan Goleman.

4. *Cultural Intelligence: Individual Interactions across Cultures,* 2003. P. Christopher Earley and Soon Ang.

5. *Leading with Cultural Intelligence*, 2015, David Livermore.

6. *Leading with Cultural Intelligence*, 2nd Edition, 2015, David Livermore.

7. *Cultural Intelligence: The Essential Intelligence for the 21st Century*, 2015, the SHRM Foundation's Effective Practice Guideline Series.

8. *Good to Great*, 2001, James C. Collins.

9. *What Motivates Me: Put Your Passions to Work*, 2019, Chester Elton and Adrian Gostick.

10. "Top 4 Reasons Diversity and Inclusion Programs Fail," March 2021, National Diversity Council, *Forbes EQ* article, Erika Johnson.

11. "Why Diversity Matters," January 2015, Vivian Hunt, Dennis Layton, and Sara Prince of McKinsey & Co.

12. "Why Diversity Programs Fail," August 2016, Frank Dobbin and Alexandra Kalev, *Harvard Business Review.*

13. "Attracting and Retaining the Right Talent," 2017, Scott Keller, McKinsey & Company.

14. "The Real Secret to Retaining Talent. The Subtle Art of Making People Feel Special," April 2022, Roger Martin, *Harvard Business Review*.

15. "How to Show White Men That Diversity and Inclusion Efforts Need Them," October 2019, Lily Zheng, *Harvard Business Review*.

16. "The Board's Role in Corporate Culture," 2019, Rick Hoel, Diligent Insights.

17. Nicole Standford, Deloitte & Touche LLP, 2018, *Wall Street Journal*.

18. "Five Ways to Enhance Board Oversight of Culture," May 2019, Joe Dettmann and Stephen Klemash, published by EY.

19. "The Importance of Brand Reputation: 20 Years to Build, Five Minutes to Ruin," December 2019, Paul Blanchard, *Forbes*.

RESOURCES

The Legacy Leader Series of Books by Anthony Lopez

The Legacy Leader: Leadership With A Purpose, 2003.

Breakthrough Thinking: The Legacy Leader's Role in Driving Innovation, 2005.

The Leader's Lobotomy: The Legacy Leader Avoids Promotion-Induced Amnesia, 2008.

The Legacy Leader: Leadership with a Purpose, 2nd Edition, 2010.

The Leader in the Mirror: The Legacy Leader's Critical Self-Assessment, 2011.

LEGACYWOMAN: The Legacy Leader as SuperHero, 2018.

ABOUT THE AUTHOR

ANTHONY LOPEZ

Anthony Lopez is the founder and CEO at L&L Advisors, a leadership and management consulting firm. He began his professional career as a captain in the Air Force. In 1991, he began his corporate career with Johnson & Johnson. While at J&J, he held leadership and executive positions in ETHICON and DePuy. He also served as chairperson for the Hispanic Organization For Leadership & Achievement. From 2009 to 2011, Tony was the SVP and GM for Respiratory in CareFusion (a $750 million business). From 2011 to 2017, he served as president for medical solutions at Ansell Healthcare. From 2017-2018, he was CEO and managing director of AZZUR Group. Tony is chairman-emeritus of the PROSPANICA board of directors and served a term on the PROSPANICA Foundation board. He also served on the board of advisors for CulturIntel Inc., Touchland Inc., and MAS Global Consulting. He is currently on the executive advisory board of NextPhase+ Capital. He holds a BS in electrical engineering and an MS in engineering management, and is a graduate of the Department of Defense Equal Opportunity Management Institute. He is a National Association of Corporate Directors (NACD) scholar and a member of the Latino Corporate Directors Association.

Tony is a sought-after speaker and expert on leadership and management topics. He has presented to audiences throughout the United States,

Latin America, Europe, and Asia, and thousands of people have attended his presentations. Tony is the author of *The Legacy Leader* (1st and 2nd editions), *Breakthrough Thinking: The Legacy Leader's Role in Driving Innovation*, *The Leader's Lobotomy: The Legacy Leader Avoids Promotion-Induced Amnesia*, *The Leader in the Mirror: The Legacy Leader's Critical Self-Assessment*, "The Diversity Engagement Model: From Awareness to Action" (published in the *Journal for Hispanic Business Research*, October 2008), and *LEGACYWOMAN: The Legacy Leader as SuperHero*. He is also the author of *See You at the Wake: Healing Relationships before It's Too Late* and *Jag: Christian Lessons from My Golden Retriever*. He can be reached via L&L's website, www.legacyleader.net, or directly via e-mail at alopez@ legacyleader.net.

ABOUT THE FOREWORD'S AUTHOR

YVONNE GARCIA

Yvonne Garcia serves as chief of staff to State Street's chairman and CEO, Ron O'Hanley, as global head of internal communications and as head of the CEO Experience Program. Before these roles, Yvonne led State Street's Global Client Solutions and Implementation team within Investment Management Services (IMS). Prior to State Street, Yvonne served as director of marketing and distribution strategy for Liberty Mutual and as vice president for Bank of America's China Construction Bank Strategic Assistance Program. As an active leader of local and national communities, Yvonne served as the chairwoman for ALPFA, the largest Latino professional organization in the country. She is also the cofounding chair of Milagros Para Niños. She was appointed by Massachusetts Governor Charlie Baker to serve on the state's Latino Advisory Commission Board and was also appointed as the chairwoman for the Greater Boston Chamber's Women's Network. Yvonne holds an MBA from Boston University in finance and marketing and a BA from SUNY Albany. She was also awarded an honorary doctorate of humane letters from Cambridge College in Boston and most recently an honorary doctorate of commerce from New England School of Business.

Printed in the United States
by Baker & Taylor Publisher Services